KA

KARUKKU

SECOND EDITION

BAMA

Translated from Tamil by
Lakshmi Holmström

Edited by
Mini Krishnan

OXFORD
UNIVERSITY PRESS

OXFORD
UNIVERSITY PRESS

Oxford University Press is a department of the University of Oxford.
It furthers the University's objective of excellence in research, scholarship,
and education by publishing worldwide. Oxford is a registered trademark of
Oxford University Press in the UK and in certain other countries

Published in India by
Oxford University Press
2/11 Ground floor, Ansari Road, Daryaganj, New Delhi 110002, India

First edition published by
Macmillan India Limited in 2000
Second edition published by
Oxford University Press in 2012
Oxford India Paperbacks in 2014
Tenth impression 2017

ISBN-13: 978-0-19-945041-1
ISBN-10: 0-19-945041-2

Typeset in 11.5/16 Venetian301 Dm BT
by Excellent Laser Typesetters, Pitampura, Delhi 110 034
Printed in India by Replika Press Pvt. Ltd.

MR. Omayal Achi MR. Arunachalam Trust was set up in 1976 to further
education and health care, particularly in rural areas. The MR. AR Educational
Society was later established by the Trust. One of the Society's activities is
to sponsor Indian literature. This translation is entirely funded by the
MR. AR Educational Society as part of its aims.

For
Mark

Contents

Ten Years Later

The year 1992 saw an extremely important turning point in my life. After seven years of living in the convent, on 8 November 1992, I left behind my life of renunciation and came out into the world. After that, I wrote my book, *Karukku*. That book was written as a means of healing my inward wounds; I had no other motive. Yes, it had unexpected results. It influenced people in many different ways. *Karukku* made me realize how potent a book can be. My parents read it. They understood me a little more. My siblings read it. They could comprehend the pain I had experienced in my life. My friends read it. They praised it because it was a new kind of writing. People from my village read it. Although they were hostile at first, they realized that it was necessary. They rejoiced and encouraged me. Many Dalits read it and said it gave them strength. Literary critics read it and analysed it, asking each other how to categorize it. They decided, finally, that it was a new genre in Tamil literature. Many praised it, many scorned it. After all the noise had died down ...

IN THE YEAR 2000 ...

Mini Krishnan was editor at Macmillan India at the time. Through her efforts, *Karukku* came out as a Macmillan publication, translated into English by Lakshmi Holmström. Following this, *Karukku* came to the attention of a national, and then international, readership. The next year, it won the Crossword Award. Then it was translated into other languages such as Malayalam, Telugu, and Kannada, in all of which it was well received. Students from different disciplines studied it, both in English and in Tamil; they continue to do so.

NOW, IN THE YEAR 2011 ...

During the past ten years, *Karukku* has journeyed widely. Many universities and colleges have used it as a textbook for different subjects such as Marginal Literature, Literature in Translation, Autobiography, Feminist Literature, and Dalit Literature. Many students have used it as research material for a number of different topics. During this same period, many fine pieces of literature and art were written and created by Dalits: poetry, novels, short fiction, short films, essays, and plays. Many of these have been translated into English as well. Dalit writing has flourished. A new generation of artists and writers has enriched Dalit Literature.

   Karukku, written by a wounded self, has not been dissolved in the stream of time. On the contrary, it has been a means of relieving the pain of others who were wounded. *Karukku* has been of comfort to many who have been brought low, and who suffer the pain of caste discrimination, untouchability, poverty, and destitution; it has given them courage and helped them to love life once more. *Karukku* stands as a means of strength to the multitudes whose identities have been destroyed and denied. During these ten years, it has reminded its readers not only that Truth alone is victorious, but that only the Truth is the Truth. *Karukku* has enabled many to raise their voices and proclaim, 'My language, my culture, my life is praiseworthy, it is excellent.' *Karukku* insists only on a humanism which crosses all boundaries; the truths it tells may be bitter to some, to some they may be ridiculous. The book stands past such criticism and speaks for itself. Its second edition, brought out by Oxford University Press (OUP), gives me boundless joy. On this happy occasion, I think of all those who have been instrumental in bringing it about, with love and gratitude.

The very same Mini Krishnan, who arranged for the publication of Lakshmi Holmström's English translation of *Karukku* in the year 2000, has worked with intense determination to bring out this second, revised and augmented edition, again with Lakshmi's help. I have been astonished by Mini's extraordinary patience, her profound sense of dedication, and her hard work. I feel there are no words to thank her for all her endeavours towards publishing Dalit writing in English translation from many different languages; and for doing this as her contribution to the liberation of those who have been marginalized by society. The effort she has made in order to bring out this second edition has been enormous. She has shared all the critical reviews of *Karukku* with me, encouraged and enthused me. I take great pleasure and pride in thanking her. To her I owe my love and gratitude forever. I described myself in *Karukku* as a bird whose wings had been clipped; I now feel like a falcon that treads the air, high in the skies. I have to say that Mini is among those who have enabled me to spread my wings and fly.

Next, Lakshmi Holmström. I know very well the care and attention she took over the translation in the year 2000. Through innumerable letters, direct meetings, and telephonic conversations she checked and clarified the text, and worked hard to bring out a beautiful translation. Once again she has translated the additional note that I have written for this edition. Amidst great pressure of work, she has re-read the text carefully, revising it where necessary, making it shine even more. I owe her my love and thanks.

I also offer my heartfelt thanks to all those at OUP for this fine edition of *Karukku*.

Uthiramerur   BAMA
2011

Translator's Note to the Second Edition

When *Karukku* was awarded the Crossword Award for translation in 2001, I was thousands of miles away, unable to attend this momentous occasion. Clearly, though, it had made literary history: a Dalit autobiography overtook mainstream writing, perhaps for the first time. Seven years later, in May 2008, both Bama and I attended the Annual Tamil Studies Conference, held at Toronto University. Bama was one of the two keynote speakers that year, and it was my privilege to introduce her on that occasion. The theme of the conference that year was 'Being Tamil', and Bama spoke on 'Being Tamil, Being Dalit'. The large lecture theatre was packed to overflowing, particularly with younger people of Sri Lankan origin. Toronto has a large diaspora of Sri Lankan Tamils, many of them political refugees, and for this audience, on the threshold of the last year of a brutal ethnic war, an exploration of what being Tamil means had a special resonance.

Bama, as usual, spoke from the heart—as she speaks in *Karukku*—directly, openly, courageously, with the self confidence and composure she has gained increasingly, since *Karukku* was first published in 2000. At the end of her talk everyone there rose to their feet spontaneously and gave her a resounding standing ovation. It was surely one of the most memorable moments of my life.

I recall this incident here because it brings home vividly, how accessible all of Bama's work, especially *Karukku,* has proved to be to an international readership. *Karukku* was written out of a specific experience, the experience of a Tamil Dalit Christian woman. Yet it has a universality at its core which questions all oppressions, disturbs all complacencies, and, reaching out, empowers all those who have suffered different oppressions. It is precisely because it tells the story of Bama's personal struggle to find her identity that *Karukku* also argues so powerfully against patriarchy and caste oppression. In the ten years since it first went into English translation, it has appealed to a variety of scholars, but most of all to the ordinary reader.

It is a privilege for me to join Bama and Mini Krishnan once more, in the task of completing the story which the author did not—perhaps could not—tell those many years ago. It is important for her to tell it now, and for us to listen.

2011   LAKSHMI HOLMSTRÖM

Introduction

'Bama' is the pen-name of a Tamil Dalit woman from a Roman Catholic family. She has published three full-length works of prose: her autobiography, *Karukku* (1992), two novels, *Sangati* (1994) and *Vanmam* (2002), and three collections of short stories, *Kisumbukkaran* (1996), *Oru Thathavum Erumayum* (2003), and *Kondattam* (2009).

Karukku means palmyra leaves, that, with their serrated edges on both sides, are like double-edged swords. By a felicitous pun, the Tamil word karukku, containing the word *karu*, embryo or seed, also means freshness, newness. In her preface, Bama draws attention to the symbol, and refers to the words in Hebrews (New Testament), 'For the word of God is living and active, sharper than any two-edged sword, piercing to the division of soul and spirit, of joints and marrow, and discerning the thoughts and intentions of the heart' (Hebrews 4:12).

Karukku is the first autobiography of its kind to appear in Tamil, for Dalit writing in this language has not produced the spate of autobiographies which have appeared, for example, in Marathi. It is also in many ways an unusual autobiography. It grows out of a particular moment: a personal crisis and watershed in the author's life which drives her to make sense of her life as woman, a Christian, and a Dalit. Many Tamil authors, both men and women, use the convention of writing under a pseudonym. In this case, though, this convention adds to the work's strange paradox of reticence and familiarity. It eschews the 'confessional' mode, leaving out many personal details. The protagonist is never named. The events of Bama's life are not arranged according to a simple, linear, or chronological order, as with most autobiographies, but rather, reflected upon in different ways, repeated from different perspectives, grouped under different themes, for example, Work, Games and Recreation, Education, Belief, and so on. It is her driving quest for integrity as a Dalit and a Christian that shapes the book and gives it its polemic.

The argument of the book is to do with the arc of the narrator's spiritual development both through the nurturing of her belief as a Catholic, and her gradual realization of herself as a Dalit. We are given a full picture of the way in which the Church ordered and influenced the lives of the Dalit Catholics. Every aspect of the child's life is imbued with the Christian religion. The day is ordered by religious ritual. The year is punctuated by religious processions and festivals which become part of the natural yearly cycle of crops and seasons. However, parallel to this religious life runs a socio-political self-education that takes off from the revelatory moment when she first understands what untouchability means. It is this double perspective that enables her to understand the deep rift between Christian beliefs and practice.

Bama's re-reading and interpretation of the Christian scriptures as an adult enables her to carve out both a social vision and a message of hope for Dalits by emphasizing the revolutionary aspects of Christianity, the values of equality, social justice, and love towards all. Her own life experiences urge her towards actively engaging in alleviating the sufferings of the oppressed. When she becomes a nun, it is in the stubborn hope that she will have a chance to put these aspirations into effect. She discovers, however, that the perspectives of the convent and the Church are different from hers. The story of that conflict and its resolution forms the core of *Karukku*.

In the end, Bama makes the only choice possible for her. But she also sees the beginnings of an important change, if not in the Church's practice, then in the gradually growing awareness among Dalits of their own oppression:

But Dalits have also understood that God is not like this, has not spoken like this. They have become aware that they too were created in the likeness of God. There is a new strength within them, urging them to reclaim that likeness which has been repressed, ruined, and obliterated; and to begin to live with honour and respect and love of all humankind. To my mind, that alone is true devotion.

Clearly she understands that her own experience is part of a larger movement among Dalits. Yet, it is interesting that she appears to come to this awareness of her own accord. She does not, for example, seem to have access to liberation theologians (as does Vidivelli, in a parallel autobiography, *Kalakkal*). She refers neither to Ambedkar nor to Periyar, who not only attacked the caste system, but whose remarkable speeches and writings against the oppression of women were published in 1942 under the title *Pen Yenh Adimaiyaanal?* (Why did woman become enslaved?) Nor indeed does Bama—again unlike Vidivelli—make a connection between caste and gender oppression. Not in *Karukku* at any rate; she does so, abundantly, in *Sangati* and elsewhere. *Karukku* is concerned with the single issue of caste oppression within the Catholic Church and its institutions, and presents Bama's life as a process of lonely self-discovery. Bama leaves her religious order to return to her village, where life may be insecure, but where she does not feel alienated or compromised. The tension throughout *Karukku* is between the self and the community: the narrator leaves one community (the religious order) and affirms her belonging to another (a Dalit community, particularly of women). *Sangati* takes up the story of that new community.

* * * *

Dalit writing—as the writers themselves have chosen to call it—has been seen in Tamil only in the past decade, and later than in Marathi and Kannada. It has gone hand in hand with political activism, and with critical and ideological debate, spurred on by such events as the Ambedkar centenary of 1994 and the furore following the Mandal Commission report.

The Tamil equivalent of the Marathi 'dalit' is *taazhtapattor*, used in this specific sense by Bharati Dasan in the 1930s, when he was working for the Self Respect Movement. He uses it in the poem '*Taazhtapattor samattuvapaattu*' ('Song for the equality of the oppressed'). Indeed the new Tamil Dalit writing constantly refers to the anti-caste, anti-religious speeches of E.V. Ramaswamy Naicker (Periyaar), founder of this movement. All the same, although the Tamil words taazhtapattor or *odukkappattor* are used in much of the literature by both writers and critics, it is significant that the preferred term is Dalit, implying militancy, an alliance with other repressed groups, and a nationwide—or even universal—identity. 'Who are Dalits? All those who are oppressed: all hill peoples, neo-Buddhists, labourers, destitute farmers, women and all those who have been exploited politically, economically or in the name of religion are Dalits' (1972 Manifesto of the Dalit Panthers, quoted in Tamil translation in Omvedt [1994]).

More recently, Raj Gautaman (1995) points to the different functions of Tamil Dalit writing, and the different local and global readerships it addressed. First, he says, it is the function of Dalit writing to awaken in every reader a consciousness of the oppressed Dalit and to share in the Dalit experience as if it were their own. (*Karukku*, he says, is a singular example of a piece of writing which achieves this.) At the same time, according to Gautaman, the new Dalit writing must be a Tamil and an Indian version of the worldwide literature of the oppressed; its politics must be an active one that fights for human rights, social justice, and equality.

I think that it would also be true to say that while much of the new Tamil Dalit writing does indeed function as Gautaman claims, and is centrally concerned with raising an awareness of the Dalit experience, Bama's work is among those (like the work of Vidivelli, Imayam, and Marku) that are exploring a changing Dalit identity. There is, in this writing, a very powerful sense of the self and the community as Dalit, which rejects outright the notion of varna and which, on the other hand, refuses to 'Sanskritize', to evaluate Dalit lifestyle according to mainstream Hindu values. There is also at the same time a powerful sense of engagement with history, of change, of changing notions of identity and belonging. Bama captures a moment that contains a paradox: she seeks an identity, but also seeks a change which means an end to that identity.

I must conclude by commenting briefly on Bama's use of language. Bama is doing something completely new in using the demotic and the colloquial routinely, as her medium for narration and even argument, not simply for reported speech. She uses a Dalit style of language which overturns the decorum and aesthetics of received upper-class, upper-caste Tamil. She breaks the rules of written grammar and spelling throughout, elides words and joins them differently, demanding a new and different pattern of reading. *Karukku* also, by using an informal speech style which addresses the reader intimately, shares with the reader the author's predicament as Dalit and Christian directly, demystifying the theological argument, and making her choice a matter of conscience.

As well as this subversion of revised Tamil, all Dalit writing is marked by certain other characteristics. It reclaims and remains close to an oral tradition made up of work-chants, folk-songs, songs sung at rites of passage, as well as proverbs—and some of this tradition belongs particularly to the woman's domain. *Karukku*, very interestingly, also tells the story of Tamil Dalit Catholicism in the vocabulary that it uses, particularly in the central chapter which describes her spiritual journey from childhood faith to homecoming after departing from the convent. There is often a layering of meaning in certain words, where a Tamilized Sanskrit word is given a new Catholic meaning. For example, Tamil *mantiram* (sacred utterance, but also popularly, magic charm or spell) from Sanskrit mantra becomes 'catechism' in Catholic use. Hence, often there is a spin or a turnaround of meaning, a freshness in some of the coinages, and different routes and slippages in the way Catholicism has been naturalized (and sometimes not) into the Tamil of the text. It is also important to note that Bama consistently uses the language of popular Catholicism, eschewing very largely, the terminology of theologians.

Bama's work is not only breaking a mainstream aesthetic, but also proposing a new one which is integral to her politics. What is demanded of the translator and reader is, in Gayatri Spivak's terms, a 'surrender to the special call of the text'. This is certainly not comfortable reading for anyone. Bama is writing in order to change hearts and minds. And as readers of her work, we are asked for nothing less than an imaginative entry into that different world of experience and its political struggle.

A part of Chapter 3 and an earlier version of the introduction appeared in *Kunapipi* (vol. XIX, no. 3 [1997]), edited by Shirley Chew. My thanks to the author Bama, and to Alies Therese of Quidenham, Norfolk, for reading this translation and commenting on it in detail.

2011   LAKSHMI HOLMSTRÖM

References

Bama, 1996, *Kisumbukkaaran*, Madurai: Ideas.

———, 1994, *Sangati*, Madurai: Ideas.

———, 1992, *Karukku*, Madurai: Ideas.

Gautaman, Raj, 1995, 'Oivaanga t vaiyillai' (We don't need haloes), *India Today*, Tamil edn., annual issue, pp. 95–8.

Imayam, 1994, *Koveri kazhudaiga* (Mules), Madras: Cre-A.

Omvedt, Gail, 1994, 'Dalit peenterkal, Tamil ilakkiyam, penkal'(Dalit Panthers, Tamil literature, women), *Nirappirikai* (Pondicherry), special edn. (November), pp. 3–7.

Periyaar, 1987, *Pen yeen aimaiyaana?* Madras: Periyaar Suyamariyaadai Pirachaara Nirumvanam.

Spivak, Gayatri Chakravorty, 1993, *Outside in the Teaching Machine*, New York: Routledge.

Tharu, Susie and K. Lalita, 1991, *Women Writing in India, Volume I: 600 BC to the Early Twentieth Century*, New Delhi: Oxford University Press.

Vidivelli, 1994, *Kalakkal*, Madurai: Ideas.

Author's Preface to the
First Edition

There are many congruities between the saw-edged palmyra karukku and my own life. Not only did I pick up the scattered palmyra karukku in the days when I was sent out to gather firewood, scratching and tearing my skin as I played with them, but later they also became the embryo and symbol that grew into this book.

The driving forces that shaped this book are many: events that occurred during many stages of my life, cutting me like karukku and making me bleed; unjust social structures that plunged me into ignorance and left me trapped and suffocating; my own desperate urge to break, throw away, and destroy these bonds; and when the chains were shattered into fragments, the blood that was spilt—all these taken together.

There are other Dalit hearts like mine, with a passionate desire to create a new society made up of justice, equality, and love. They, who have been the oppressed, are now themselves like the double-edged karukku, challenging their oppressors.

Although the author of *The Epistle to the Hebrews* (New Testament) described the Word of God as a two-edged sword, it no longer stirs the hardened hearts of the many who have sought their happiness by enslaving and disempowering others.

In order to change this state of affairs, all Dalits who have been deprived of their basic rights must function as God's word, piercing to the very heart. Instead of being more and more beaten down and blunted, they must unite, think about their rights, and battle for them.

Father Mark understood the nature and sources of this book, and urged me to write it. Not only did he encourage me to give thought to each separate topic, he supported me in the writing of it, he worked tirelessly to bring out the Tamil edition in the shape of a book, and honoured it by writing an introduction. I am indebted to him in many ways. Out of many other friends who encouraged and inspired me, I must mention Father M. Jeyaraj in particular.

1992   BAMA

Editor's Note to the
First Edition

Breaking a silence that has lasted for more generations than we can count comes Bama's *Karukku*, a text which is a life story that could lay the foundation for a course on Dalit memoirs. Part autobiography, part analysis, part manifesto, Bama's is a bold account of what life is like outside the mainstream of Indian thought and function.

'Dalit' is a Marathi word derived from Sanskrit, 'dala' meaning 'of the soil or the earth'. Another meaning is 'that which is rooted in the soil'. Extend that meaning and you have that which has been ground down.

The term has come to occupy the same range of meanings in Tamil and includes socially suppressed caste groups: all those who have, for centuries, been exploited in the name of religion and society by those in positions of power. Dalit art forms grow out of an ideology of freedom from oppression and they need wider recognition and understanding.

Readers may find Bama's exposé of certain aspects of our society shocking. No one can ignore her experience.

2000   MINI KRISHNAN

One

Our village is very beautiful. Even though you don't see much by way of progress or anything like that here, I love this place for its beauty. Although it's only a small village, many different communities live here. But before I come to castes and communities, I have a lot to say about the village itself.

The mountains range right around the village. They are lovely to look at. People say they are the Western Ghats. They have names, too, for some of the mountain peaks. One is called the Marakkaa puucchi malai. This mountain, if you look at it properly, is just like a heap of paddy. Right at the peak, perches a crag that looks exactly like a marakkaal paddy measure. That's why the mountain has that name.

On top of another peak is a Perumaal Saami temple. A temple where the Naicker community worships. This mountain is known as the Perumaara. And the Naickers' fields surrounding it are called the Perumaara fields.

There are many more rocks round about such as Nari paara, Vannaan paara, Vattala Vitthaam paara. It seems in the old days Nari paara was full of woods, crowded with foxes. People say that the foxes living there would raid the fields round about and completely ruin them. But apparently this has not happened so much in recent times. They say there is a tank at the top of Vannaan paara. In the past, the Vannaan boys would wash clothes there, steaming and whitening them, but today they don't go that far. And Vattala Vitthaam paara is so named because Vattala Vittha Naicker has his fields there. The mountains encircle the village, making a kind of border.

Most of our people are agricultural labourers. When there is no call for work in the fields, they go up to the woods on the mountains, and make a living by gathering firewood and selling it. People from the better-off castes never have such problems, though. They own fields with boundaries; they have dug wells and established pump-sets; they can work their land all year; they eat well and live in comfort in their homes. Anyway, besides wells there are any number of ponds in these parts.

In the rainy season our village becomes even more lushly beautiful. The rainwater comes bounding and leaping down the mountain slopes and fills the streams that encircle the village. At such times one can catch fish in the abundant stretches of water. All that water accumulates at last in the ponds and lakes. So that's another thing that helps agriculture.

If you look in a westward direction, the lakes and ponds stand side by side, strung together in a row: Taamara kulam (lotus pond), Baathraang kulam (named for the priests or podagar who lived nearby), Jeevaneri kamma (the lake of life), Aiyar kulam (pond of the Aiyars), Periya kulam (the big pond), Poder kulam (probably also named for the podagar), Vilraang kulam. The pond nearest our street has two names. The shore nearest us is Anupaang kulam. The opposite shore is called Vathraang kulam after the village of Vathraa.

When the rains fall heavily and the big lake fills up, our pond too normally brims over. It used to be fun to walk along the shore at such a time. When there was plenty of water, they would pull up the hatches to the canals feeding the lake, and let the water flow through. People would catch any amount of fish by placing earthen pots just where the water flowed through. The streets overflowed with fish during the season. People sold all sorts of fish like silabi kendai, paaruku kendai, keluti, ayirai, koravi, viraal. But in our own street, we mostly bought and cooked curries out of silebi kendai and paambu kendai. Because that was the cheapest we could get. The upper castes bought and ate ayirai, keluti, and viraal. But we couldn't afford to pay that much for what we ate.

When the pond was full, people sat under the shade of the banyan tree which grew on the shore, talking of the past. The wind blew fresh and cool, almost like a sea breeze. Such a sense of comfort there would be. Your eyes would almost droop into a slumber. The wind, rippling the surface of the water, made endless tiny waves, pretty to see. You could stand on the shore and watch the fish leaping. The bright fish would leap into the air, glinting in the sunlight. Water-snakes would lift their heads above the water and look about. Little boys aimed their stones at them. Padak! Quick as a flash they would disappear into the water. As soon as the man who held the fishing rights for the pond went off for his meal of kanji or whatever, everyone, big and small, would whip out their fishing rods. If you used the earthworms from rubbish heaps as bait, then you could catch fish very easily. People would light small fires of straw, right there on the shore, and roast the newly caught fish. It used to taste delicious. But if ever the caretaker caught sight of us, then that was it. He'd confiscate all the fish and smash up the rods as well. Small children splashed about and played in the water like little tadpoles throughout the hot afternoons. Next to them, buffaloes bathed pleasurably. Some of the more daring and mischievous boys climbed onto a buffalo's back and rode as far as the middle of the pond and back. Even an infant, born just the other day, tumbled naked in the water.

There is a small water-source in the middle of the lake, surrounded by banyan trees. Even when the lake dried out, the little pond at its centre always held water. When the lake floor was dry, they would grow something or other there—perhaps cucumber, or some millet like cholam or kambu. If you went there and pulled off a cucumber to eat, its touch upon the tongue was wonderful on a hot day. In any case there is a special taste to food snatched by stealth.

At dawn and at dusk, the eastern and western skies are splendid to see. When we used to go out in the early morning to relieve ourselves, a bright red sun, huge and round, would wake up in the east and climb into the sky. It would make its way, peering between the trees, glowing, its light spilling and sparkling. And in the same way, at evening time, when it went and dropped through the mountains, all the fields round about would be luminous with a yellow light. A cool southern breeze would blow through the fields. The crops glowing, swaying in the breeze, filled the heart with delight. To look at the light in the western sky was like looking upon a vision of God. And at that very moment herons and crows and all the other birds would wing their way home to their nests.

To the west of our village, there is a place we call the mandavam. It's a pillared structure, now in ruins. The Muniappasaami shrine is right there. It is actually at quite some distance from our street. Yet people would go that far, five or six miles to the fields and building there, in order to scrape together a living. Once a year there was a festival there at the Muniappasaami temple, when offerings of food and money were made. It was said that a man called Bondan, from the North Street of our part of the village, went there once and stole the money offering, and untied the temple bell and carried it away. This was a man who would steal anything. Yet people were shocked that he had gone and burgled—of all places—the Muniyaandi shrine.

From that day, people said that as night-time drew near, Muniyaandi would walk along the rubbish tip at our street, burning torch in hand, furious. They said that he walked along, calling out, 'Return my offering to me, put back my bell, otherwise I will burn down this entire street until nothing is left but ashes.' Many people had caught sight of him as he did this. But nobody understood what it was all about. Later when they started asking each other, Bondan's father, Savurinaayagam Thaattha told everyone what had happened. Then they all joined together and insisted that Bondan should return the money and replace the temple bell. He did as he was told, going to the mandavam with the mark of the cross upon him to return the bell and the offering money. After that the terrible Devil never came down our street again.

There used to be lots of stories about this Bondan-Maama. His chief means of livelihood was stealing limes, coconuts, and mangoes from the landowning families' gardens and groves and then selling them. Once, at midnight, he climbed a coconut palm to pluck some coconuts. As he gradually moved upwards from the base of the coconut palm, a strange form slid down its trunk from above. He was perplexed for awhile, wondering who it could be. Then, in a flash realizing it was a pey tormenting him, he clambered down hastily, and dashed off to another grove.

Another time, just as he was coming along, having helped himself liberally to a sackful of mangoes, he saw the caretaker ahead of him. There was no way he could escape, so he decided to jump into a nearby well and pass the time there, hiding his bundle under water. It was rather like the tale of the man who feared the sun and jumped into a pan of boiling water, though. Because, once he was in the well, a cobra suddenly spread its hood and made to bite him. They say it came towards him, hood raised, hissing. It was pitch dark, besides. Somehow he kept the cobra at bay until the watchman moved away from there, and then he came home safe and sound with his bundle.

Then, on another occasion when he was out on his raids, a snake bit him right on his big toe. And it was no ordinary snake either, but a king cobra. Anyone else would have died of fright there and then. This man, though, immediately struck a match, burnt out the spot, cut away the toe with his sickle, then finished his raid and returned. Such a sharp fellow he was.

It was said that he even managed to survive an encounter with an 'ayyangaatchi' troupe. An ayyangaatchi troupe, they used to say, was a crowd of peys, large and small, coming along with lighted torches. People hardly ever caught sight of them. If anybody saw them, there was no escape. The merest glimpse would induce fever, frightful diarrhoea, and eventual death. But Bondan got away with it.

Most of the land belonged to the Naicker community. Each Naicker's fields were spread over many miles. The fields in every direction had their own names. There was one field called Olivizhikkaadu, the field of awakening sound. They said it was an open ground where everything that was said aloud, echoed. There were other fields known as Mandavak kaadu, Otthaalu kaadu, Chadayaalu kaadu, and the field with the lotus pond. Our people knew all the fields by their names and turned up exactly where they were required to work. Otthaalu field was called that because a single banyan tree, an aalu, stood at its centre. Chadayaalu field had banyan trees with aerial roots which fell like plaited hair and fixed themselves into the earth.

Just at the entrance to the village there is a small bus stand. This is the terminus. The bus will take you no further. It is as if our entire world ended there. Beyond that, there is a stream. If it rains, it runs full of water. If not, it is nothing but a stinking shit-field. To the left there is a small settlement of ten to twenty houses, known as Odapatti. It is full of Nadars who climb palmyra palms for a living. To the right there are the Koravar who sweep streets, and then the leather-working Chakkiliyar. Some distance away there are the Kusavar who make earthenware pots. Next to that comes the Palla settlement. Then, immediately adjacent to that is where we live, the Paraya settlement. To the east of the village lies the cemetery. We live just next to that.

Apart from us, following one after the other in a series, there were the streets of the Thevar, Chettiyaar, Aasaari, and Nadar. Beyond that were the Naicker streets. The Udaiyaar, too, had a small settlement there for themselves. I don't know how it came about that the upper-caste communities and the lower caste-communities were separated like this into different parts of the village. But they kept themselves to their part of the village, and we stayed in ours. We only went to their side if we had work to do there. But they never, ever, came to our parts. The post office, the panchayat board, the milk-depot, the big shops, the church, the schools—all these stood in their streets. So why would they need to come to our area? Besides, there was a big school in the Naicker street which was meant only for the upper-caste children.

There were five streets that made up the part where our community lived: South Street, Middle Street, North Street, East Street, and Olatharapatti Street. Row upon row of houses. Three-quarters of them were cottages with palmyra-thatched roofs. In between, a few with tiled roofs. Here and there, a few houses of lime and plaster. Those were the houses of the government employees.

In the streets, the children used to wander, bare-bottomed, both boys and girls. Even if a few boys wore pants, they would usually have slipped down, hardly covering what they were supposed to cover.

Their bottoms were never as big as their bellies, so their pants would not stay up. The moment it struck twelve, they'd rush off plate in hand, even the tiniest crab-like ones, for their free meal. The church bell struck the hour at twelve. That was the signal.

In the afternoon, after five o'clock, the streets were all noise and bustle. Men and women would be out there, shouting and yelling. Usually there were fights going on among those who waited their turn at the single water pump. It took such an age to fill a single water pot, even if you worked the pump strenuously. But the quarrels and fights going on there really made you laugh.

Once, it seems, a woman called Gnanappu, from the Middle Street, left her bucket to mark her place in the queue and went off on some chore or other. Before she returned, the others took her bucket away and placed it at the end of the queue. It seems she stood her ground stubbornly, saying, 'How dare you chuck away my *bycket*?' Everyone there burst out laughing because she kept on saying 'bycket' for 'bucket'. It seems she was incensed and started cursing and calling them names, saying, 'You are only fit to collect sniggers and slippers like Chakkili boys.'

The names you heard along our streets would really surprise you. People's baptismal names, given at church, were one thing; the names we used in the street were quite another. One child's name was Munkovam, short temper. A woman was called Midday-masala. One day she ground masala at midday, and made a curry. Usually, in our street, no one cooked at noon. It was only in the evening that people cooked rice, made a curry; at other times it was always kuuzh, millet-porridge. So grinding masala at noon-time was a real surprise to us. A certain child who was very dark-skinned and plump was named Murugan-spring pig. It seems that pigs wandered about, well-fed and plump, by the spring of Murugan; that's why. There was a woman who leaked all over her legs when she relieved herself; she was called Kazhinja, Leaky. A small girl who went off to practise swimming in the well, but could only manage to float, was promptly named Medenda, Floater. Yet another woman used to go about chasing crows away when she was a small child. The name stuck to her, Kaakkaa, Crow. I could go on and on. Konnavaachi (Starer), Deaf one, Dumbo, Crazy, Severiyaa (Xavier), Black ant, Manacchi (Flat nose), Uzhamuki (Running nose), Green nose, Needle-bum. All sorts of names like that.

There was no shortage of nicknames for boys either. There were lots of those too, in fact. One boy was called Dal-bum. Nobody knew why. Another one was called Kalkundaan (Boulder). Yet another who used to say 'endrayya' instead of 'engayya' as a small boy, was stuck with the name 'Endrayya'. And the little chap who used to say 'teppa tuuzhu' for 'keppa kuuzhu' was called Teppa Tuuzhu even when he grew up. And so I could go on with names like Black mouth, Nezhucchaan (Staggerer), Belly button, Kaaman (Jack of all trades), Bondan (Snatcher), Vidvi (Idiot), Naadodi (Wanderer), Idiot, and Half-ear.

This fellow called Kaaman lived quite near our house. It seems his real name was Maria-Lourdes. Nobody knew who gave him his nickname, nor why. Anyhow, he was called this from the time he was a small child. Now he would be about twenty, twenty-five, perhaps. Until about a year ago, he wouldn't do any work, but only wandered about the streets. If anyone asked him to go to the shops for them, he'd do it. Or if they asked him to go and post a letter at the post office, he'd go. If ever he did this, people would give him five or ten paise. He'd buy some food out of that, eat some gruel, and stretch out along the front ledge of our cottages, without a care all day, until milking time in the evening. Some people called him a

simpleton. Some said he was half crazy. A strange melancholic kind
of boy he was.

And then everything changed. Suddenly he began to go to work
somewhere, regularly. Only no one seemed to know what exactly it was
he did. Anyhow, he had been given a khaki uniform for his work. On
Sundays he would appear at church in the very same uniform. There
wasn't a single person in village who didn't laugh at those khaki pants
and shirt. Then, after a while, all that disappeared, and he was back
again, lying on our front ledges like a broody hen sitting on eggs. All
of a sudden, for some reason, he began to take on coolie work like
everyone else. Nowadays he goes to work regularly. And for the past
four or five months, he has been wanting to get married, it seems. If
anybody asks him, 'Who's going to give their daughter to you, of all
people?' he will ask them in his turn, 'Why, what's wrong with me?
Why won't they give me their girl?' People say that nobody in this
village is likely to give him their daughter or their money; if he finds
a girl elsewhere, he'll be lucky.

Some folk say that if by chance he does get married, he'll make
quite a good job of cooking the food. They say he can make a rice-
gruel as well as any woman can. But he'll cook the rice, eat it all by
himself, and leave the pots washed clean. His own mother says that! It
seems he can polish off half a padi of rice all by himself. Anyway, we
have all sorts of people like this. You could write a whole book about
each of them.

* * * *

There's a village to the north of us. It's called Archanaavaraam. That's
where you'll find the Nallathanga temple. Nallathangaal is very famous
in our parts. If you ask some of the older folk, they'll tell you her
story in great detail and with a lot of fervour.

In the old days there were two people in this village: one, the elder brother, the other, the younger sister. As their parents were dead, the brother looked after the little girl, and in due course got her married to someone from Maanaamarutai or thereabouts. After he had given her away, he too found himself a wife. But the woman he married was a vain and conceited woman; she could never allow anyone to go anywhere near him.

After some time, there was a terrible famine in Maanaamarutai, where Nallathangaal had gone after she married. By this time, Nallathangaal had borne seven children, one after another. After the birth of each child she had written to her brother. The vain and conceited sister-in-law intercepted each letter and flung it into the fire. So the elder brother had not got any news of his sister. He was always worrying about her; how she was, what was happening to her.

When Maanaamarutai was suffering from the famine, Nallathangaal wrote yet another letter to her brother, telling him about her pitiable condition. By some kind god's mercy, the brother happened to be at home at the right time. He read the letter and sobbed his heart out like a woman. When he asked his wife where all his sister's previous letters had gone, she deceived him with all sorts of fibs, and somehow got round him. Anyway, the elder brother set off immediately for Maanaamarutai and brought away Nallathangaal and her seven children. As they neared his village, he told Nallathangaal to go on ahead, while he himself went to buy some necessary household things. When Muuli Alangaari saw Nallathangaal approaching with her seven children, she ran and locked all the doors to the house so that no one could come in. Nallathangaal approached the door and knocked on it several times, and said at last, 'If I have been a true and faithful wife, this door will open at once.' And sure enough, it did.

She called her children to her, went in, and sat down. The children, who had walked in the heat for a long time, were so ravenous that they fell upon everything they could find in the house, and began to eat with great relish. The vain and conceited one was furious when she saw this. She plucked away the food from the little ones and drove them all out. Nallathangaal gathered her children about her, and not knowing what to do or how to survive, pushed all seven of them into a nearby well, and then jumped in after them and perished. And when she was throwing the children into the well, the last little one escaped and ran away. He rushed off and took refuge with a shepherd. But Nallathangaal ran after him, dragged him away from the shepherd, flung him into the water, and leapt in herself.

When the elder brother came home with his purchases, he found his wife alone at home. When he asked her where Nallathangaal and the children were, she lied that they had not been seen at all. He ran out of the house immediately and searched everywhere. At last the shepherd told him the whole story. At once the elder brother understood everything. When he realized what his wife, in her cruelty, had done to his little sister, he carried Muuli Alangaari to the burning kiln, threw her inside, and killed her. Then he made statues of Nallathangaal and her seven children, and placed them in a shrine which he built right next to the well. He made a statue of the shepherd too. And then he himself died. I don't know whether all this really happened or not. But to this day, the well, the temple, and the statues are all still there.

Two

When I was studying in the third class, I hadn't yet heard people speak openly of untouchability. But I had already seen, felt, experienced, and been humiliated by what it is.

I was walking home from school one day, an old bag hanging from my shoulder. It was actually possible to walk the distance in ten minutes. But usually it would take me thirty minutes at the very least to reach home. It would take me from half an hour to an hour to dawdle along, watching all the fun and games that were going on, all the entertaining novelties and oddities in the streets, the shops, and the bazaar.

The performing monkey; the snake which the snake charmer kept in its box and displayed from time to time; the cyclist who had not got off his bike for three days, and who kept pedalling as hard as he could from break of day; the rupee notes that were pinned on to his shirt to spur him on; the merry-go-rounds and giant wheels; the Maariyaata temple, the huge bell hanging there; the Pongal offerings being cooked in front of the temple; the dried-fish stall by the statue of Gandhi; the sweet stall, the stall selling fried snacks, and all the other shops next to each other; the street light always demonstrating how it could change from blue to violet; the narikkuravan hunter-gypsy with his wild lemur in cages, selling needles, clay beads, and instruments for cleaning out the ears—oh, I could go on and on. Each thing would pull me to a standstill and not allow me to go any further.

At times, people from various political parties would arrive, put up a stage, and harangue us through their mikes. Then there might be a street play, or a puppet show, or a 'no magic, no miracle' stunt performance. All these would happen from time to time. But almost certainly there would be some entertainment or the other going on.

Even otherwise, there were the coffee clubs in the bazaar: the way each waiter cooled the coffee, lifting a tumbler high up and pouring its contents into a tumbler held in his other hand. Or the way some people sat in front of the shops chopping up onion, their eyes turned elsewhere so that they would not smart. Or the almond tree growing there and its fruit which was occasionally blown down by the wind. All these sights taken together would tether my legs and stop me from going home.

And then, according to the season, there would be mango, cucumber, sugar cane, sweet potato, palm-shoots, gram, palm-syrup and palm-fruit, kela-pazham, and jackfruit. Every day I would see people selling sweet and savoury fried snacks, paniyaaram, payasam, halva, boiled tamarind seeds, and iced lollies.

Gazing at all this, one day, I crossed the street of the Pallas and came to my street, the street of the Parayas, that is, my bag slung over my shoulder. At the opposite corner, though, a threshing floor had been set up, and the Naicker watched the proceedings, seated on a piece of sacking spread over a stone ledge. Our people were hard at work, driving cattle in pairs, round and round, to tread out the grain from the straw. The animals were muzzled so that they wouldn't help themselves to the straw. I stood for a while there, watching the fun.

Just then, an elder of our street came along from the direction of the bazaar. The manner in which he was walking along made me want to double up. I wanted to shriek with laughter at the sight of such a big man carrying a small packet in that fashion. I guessed there was something like vadai or green banana bhajji in the packet, because the wrapping paper was stained with oil. He came along, holding out the packet by its string, without touching it. I stood there thinking to myself, if he holds it like that, won't the package come undone, and the vadais fall out?

The elder went straight up to the Naicker, bowed low and extended the packet towards him, cupping the hand that held the string with his other hand. Naicker opened the parcel and began to eat the vadais.

After I had watched all this, at last I went home. My elder brother was there. I told him the story in all its comic detail. I fell about with laughter at the memory of a big man, and an elder at that, making such a game out of carrying the parcel. But Annan was not amused. Annan told me the man wasn't being funny when he carried the package like that. He said everybody believed that Naickers were upper caste, and therefore must not touch Parayas. If they did, they would be polluted. That's why he had to carry the package by its string.

When I heard this, I didn't want to laugh any more, and I felt terribly sad. How could they believe that it was disgusting if a Paraya held that package in his hands, even though the vadai had been wrapped first in a banana leaf, and then parcelled in paper? I felt so provoked and angry that I wanted to go and touch those wretched vadais myself, straightaway. Why should we have to fetch and carry for these people, I wondered. Such an important elder of ours goes off meekly to the shops to fetch snacks and hands them over reverently, bowing and shrinking, to this fellow who just sits there and stuffs them into his mouth. The thought of it infuriated me. How was it that these fellows thought so much of themselves? Because they had scraped four coins together, did that mean they must lose all human feelings? What did it mean when they called us 'Paraya'? Had the name become that obscene? But we too are human beings. Our people should never run these petty errands for these fellows. We should work in their fields, take home our wages, and leave it at that.

Both my grandmothers worked as servants for Naicker families. In the case of one of them, when she was working in the fields, even tiny children, born the other day, would call her by her name and order her about, just because they belonged to the Naicker caste. And this grandmother, like all the other labourers, would call the little boy Ayya, Master, and run about to do his bidding. It was shameful to see them do this. Even the way they were given their drinking water was disquieting to watch. The Naicker women would pour out the water from a height of four feet, while Paatti and the others received and drank it with cupped hands held to their mouths. I always felt terrible when I watched this. My other Paatti was the same. As soon as dawn broke, she would go to the Naicker houses, sweep out the cowshed, collect up the dung and dirt, and then bring home the left-over rice and curry from the previous evening. And for some reason she would behave as if she had been handed the nectar of the gods.

It was a long time before I realized that Paatti was bringing home the unwanted food that the Naickers were ready to throw away. One day I went with Paatti to the Naicker house. After she had finished all her filthy chores, Paatti placed the vessel that she had brought with her, by the side of the drain. The Naicker lady came out with her leftovers, leaned out from some distance and tipped them into Paatti's vessel, and went away. Her vessel, it seemed, must not touch Paatti's; it would be polluted. Sometime later, I said to Paatti she should not lay herself open to such behaviour; it was ugly to see. What Paatti said to me in return was this: These people are the maharajas who feed us our rice. Without them, how will we survive? Haven't they been upper caste from generation to generation, and haven't we been lower caste? Can we change this?

My elder brother, who was studying at a university, came home for the holidays. He would often go to the library in our neighbouring village in order to borrow books. He was on his way home one day, walking along the banks of the irrigation tank. One of the Naicker men came up behind him. He thought my Annan looked unfamiliar, and so he asked, 'Who are you, appa, what's your name?' Annan told him his name. Immediately the other man asked, 'Thambi, on which street do you live?' The point of this was that if he knew on which street we lived, he would know our caste too. Annan's reply was sharp, like a slap in the face, 'I am a Paraya from the Cheri Street.' Then he stalked off, as fast as he could. Naicker was furious. He thought he had been humiliated. He asked someone else there, 'Who is this fellow? Look at the way he talks.' This other man explained who Annan was, by mentioning our Paatti. 'Oh, that is our Rakamma's grandson.'

The next day, when Paatti went to work, the Naicker spoke to her angrily. 'How dare your grandson talk to me so arrogantly?' Paatti managed to handle it by saying, 'See, Ayya, he's an educated lad; these college boys will talk like that.' When Annan heard this, he just laughed.

Apparently it was just the same at the library. They would look at the Paraya lads from Cheri Street in a certain way, with a certain contempt. Once, when Annan was signing out his books, he added his title, M.A., on a sudden impulse. Immediately the attendant brought him a stool to sit on, and what's more, began addressing him as 'Sir'.

Annan told me all these things. And he added, 'Because we are born into the Paraya jati, we are never given any honour or dignity or respect. We are stripped of all that. But if we study and make progress, we can throw away these indignities. So study with care, learn all you can. If you are always ahead in your lessons, people will come to you of their own accord and attach themselves to you. Work hard and learn.' The words that Annan spoke to me that day made a very deep impression on me. And I studied hard, with all my breath and being, in a frenzy almost. As Annan had urged, I stood first in my class. And because of that, many people became my friends, even though I am a Paraichi.

It was the same story at school, though. They always spoke in a bad way about people of our caste. If ever anything bad happened, they would say immediately, and without hesitation, 'It must be one of the Cheri children who did it.' About three-quarters of the children in the school were Pallar and Parayar. All the same, the priests had built the school on Nadar Street. The church too, was in the same street; so was the priests' house.

Everyone seemed to think Harijan children were contemptible. But they didn't hesitate to use us for cheap labour. So we carried water to the teacher's house; we watered the plants. We did all the chores that were needed about the school.

Then I was in the seventh class. Every day, after school, I would play with the other children of our street before going home in the evening. There were two or three children who were related to me, and other boys and girls who always played together as a group.

One day, we were playing on the big neem tree in front of the school, hanging like bats, upside down from its branches. After a while, we started on another game—running right up the coconut palm and touching its tip. The coconut palm grew slantwise, at a convenient angle. If you came running along from a distance, at top speed, you could reach right to its tip and touch the coconut growing there. Spurred on by the excitement of the first few who managed to touch the coconut, those who came later grabbed it and gave it a twist before climbing down. By the time I got there, the coconut fell at my touch, dropping with a thud. It wasn't even a fully ripened coconut, just a green one, without so much as water in it. All the children were frightened and ready to scatter. Everyone said that it was I who had plucked it. Then we just left it there and ran home.

The next morning at assembly, the headmaster called out my name. 'You have shown us your true nature as a Paraya,' he said. 'You climbed the coconut tree yesterday after everybody else had gone home, and you stole a coconut. We cannot allow you inside this school. Stand outside.' I was in agony because I had been shamed and insulted in front of all the children.

The headmaster was of the Chaaliyar caste. At that time, there was a battle going on between the Chaaliyar people and us, about the cemetery. All the children eyed me in a strange way and walked off to their classes. I was in such shock and pain, I didn't know what to do. Then a teacher who lived on our street came by and advised me to go to the priest, tell him everything, and bring a letter from him to the headmaster. I went to the priest and told him the whole story in detail, and begged him to give me permission to go back to school. The priest's first response was to say, 'After all, you are from the Cheri. You might have done it. You must have done it.' The tears started welling up in my eyes, and I wept. After a long time, the priest wrote a note asking that I should be allowed to return to the school. When I took it to the headmaster, he abused me roundly, using every bad word that came to his mouth, and then told me to go to my classroom. When I entered the classroom, the entire class turned round to look at me, and I wanted to shrink into myself as I went and sat on my bench, still weeping.

I studied up to the eighth class in my village, and then went on to high school in a neighbouring town. I was very surprised when I saw the school there, the children who attended it and the clothes they wore. I felt very shy and almost fearful. It felt good just to climb the stairs and to walk into the classrooms upstairs, in such a big school. But I got used to it soon enough. And I also began to work at my studies eagerly. The children living in the hostel who were the same age as me wore smart clothes and possessed all sorts of finery like jewels and wristwatches. I thought to myself that they were, in all probability, from upper-caste families.

The Warden-Sister of our hostel could not abide low-caste or poor children. She'd get hold of us and scold us for no rhyme or reason. If a girl tended to be on the plump side, she'd get it even more. 'These people get nothing to eat at home; they come here and they grow fat,' she would say publicly. When we returned to the school after the holidays, she would say, 'Look at the Cheri children! When they stay here, they eat their fill and look as round as potatoes. But look at the state in which they come back from home—just skin and bone!' It was really embarrassing. We too paid our fees like everyone else, for our food, for this and that. Yet we had to listen to all this as well.

When I went home for holidays, if there was a Naicker woman sitting next to me in the bus, she'd immediately ask me which place I was going to, what street. As soon as I said, the Cheri, she'd get up and move off to another seat. Or she'd tell me to move elsewhere. As if I would go! I'd settle into my seat even more firmly. They'd prefer then to get up and stand all the way rather than sit next to me or to any other woman from the Cheri. They'd be polluted, apparently. This happened to me several times. When I came home and told my mother, she advised me, 'Say you are from a different caste. They'll never know.' I'd tell myself, 'But why should I pretend to these people that I'm from a different caste?' All the same, the pain I felt was not a trifling one.

Many of the children at my school were very poor at their lessons. I studied hard and got the best marks in my class. Because of this, all the children would speak to me and were friendly. Frequently I remembered what Annan had said to me when he was at home. The teachers and Sisters who taught me often encouraged me and were friendly towards me. This made me keener about my lessons. They asked me to help the children who were really backward at their lessons. I was overjoyed.

All the same, every now and then, our class teacher, or the PT teacher would ask all the Harijan children to stand up, either at assembly, or during lessons. We'd stand. They'd write down our names, and then ask us to sit down again. We felt really bad then. We'd stand in front of nearly two thousand children, hanging our heads in shame, as if we had done something wrong. Yes, it was humiliating.

I was awarded a prize for standing first among all the Harijan pupils of that district who took the government S.S.L.C. exam that year. My name was called out in assembly, and everyone clapped. My mother and I stood side by side very happily. And on that day I wasn't embarrassed to be singled out as Harijan, as the Harijan child who had gained the best marks. I was even pleased. And the other children congratulated me for doing so well. I thought, why? Is it impossible for a Harijan to study, or what? I felt a certain pride then, a desire to prove that we could study just as well as others, and to make progress.

So I finished my schooling in these parts and started my college studies at a village some distance away. I had thought that at such a big college, at such a distance away, among so many different students, nobody would bother about such things as caste. But even there, they did certainly consider caste differences. Suddenly one day a lecturer announced, 'Will Harijan students please stand; the government has arranged that Scheduled Caste students should get special tuition in the evenings.' Just two students stood up: myself, and another girl. Among the other students, a sudden rustling, a titter of contempt. I was filled with a sudden rage. At once I told the teacher that I didn't want their special tuition or anything else, and sat down. It struck me that I would not be rid of this caste business easily, whatever I studied, wherever I went.

At another time I asked for permission to go home because my younger brother and sister were to make their First Communion. It was to be for a Saturday and Sunday; these were anyway customary holidays. Even so, the Principal and the Warden joined together and were adamantly refusing to allow me to go. I grew hot with anger. I saw with my own eyes that they were giving permission for the wealthy children to go home. I lost my temper and challenged them head-on, 'How is it that you are allowing these others to go; why is it that you only refuse me?' The reply that I was given: 'What celebration can there be in your caste, for a First Communion?' They told me, in their domineering way, that they could not let me go to attend minor occasions like these. They more they spoke, the more I felt a wild rage impelling me to go, come what may. So I stood my ground obstinately. I managed to get my way at last by insisting that there cannot be different rules for different castes, only the same rules for everyone.

Anyway, I finished there and went to a different college in order to take a B.Ed. degree. It was the same story there too. Yet, because I had the education, because I had the ability, I dared to speak up for myself; I didn't care a toss about caste. Whatever the situation, I held my head high. And I completed whatever I took up, successfully. So, both teachers and students showed me a certain affection, respect. In this way, because of my education alone I managed to survive among those who spoke the language of caste-difference and discrimination.

Then I completed my education and went to work. At my first place of work, a nun asked me, 'Are you a Nadar?' I said, 'No, we are Parayar.' When I recall the expression that came over her face, I want to laugh, even now. Most of the nuns there were Telugu people. They did not care for Dalits like us. Then, what else? The next five years that I worked there were a continuous battle. I had a lot of spirit and guts at that time. The children in my class, and all the school children liked me. Many of the children there were Dalits themselves. So I was happy teaching the children and arguing with the nuns. I enjoyed standing up to the authorities and teaching with some skill and success.

I might have continued in that way. But from somewhere or other a desire came over me. It struck me overwhelmingly that these nuns collectively oppressed Dalit children and teachers so very much; why should I not become a nun too and truly help these people who are humiliated so much and kept under such strict control? The thought kept returning every day, however hard I pushed it away. So at last I resigned the teaching post that I held, and went and entered a religious order.

People I knew well, both from within the family and outside it, told me I should not leave the work I was doing. They said I could do far more useful work as a layperson than I would do as a nun. They said that caste-difference counted for a great deal within convents. But would I listen? In spite of everything they said, I entered the order. Before my decision, I had read about the woman who founded that particular order, how she had done so for the sake of the poor and lowly, lived and died for them alone. I wanted to be like her, living only for the poor and downtrodden; so I entered that particular order. But once inside the convent, it was like coming from the backwoods into a big metropolis. My first thought was that I had arrived at a place which had no connection at all with me. Then

I thought, well, I should wait and see. I was deeply troubled. But I tried hard to quieten myself.

One day, the Sister who was supervising our training, asked me in English why the birth dates were different on my degree certificate and on my christening certificate. I said that the people at my school had put down whatever birth date they chose for me because they didn't know any better. She would not believe me. Well, that would not have mattered either. But she would not leave it alone. She complained, 'You Tamil people want to get admission into schools under false pretences, changing the dates on your birth certificates.' I thought to myself, what a nuisance this is turning out to be; thus far they made us hang our heads in humiliation because of our caste; in this order being a Tamil seems to be equivalent to being a Paraya.

Then I told myself, 'Well, after all, this woman doesn't know about village life, that's why she snaps at me like this.' So a little later, I explained to her in great detail that there was no great problem about getting admission at our school; that, on the contrary, teachers visited homes and dragged their pupils out; and so there was no need to put a false date of birth in order to find a place in the school. Even after all that she insisted that I was lying. So I left it, realizing that there was no point in talking to her any more.

It was only after this that I began to understand, little by little, that in that order, Tamil people were looked upon as a lower caste. And then, among Tamils, Parayar were a separate category. Even so I continued to stay in the convent. Among those who were training with me to become nuns, every single one was anxious to find out to what caste I belonged. One day, one of them asked me straight out. When I answered her honestly, she would not believe me. So I let it go, thinking, 'What more can I do. Leave it. If you want to believe me, do so. If not, what can I do about it?'

There were only a few days left for us to finish our training and to become fully-fledged nuns. In a particular class, a Sister told us that in certain orders they would not accept Harijan women as prospective nuns and that there was even a separate order for them somewhere. I was thunderstruck. I despaired at heart, thinking, 'She tells us this now, at the last moment.' Anyhow, I thought I should ask her about it, and so I went to her and explained that I was from a Harijan family, and asked whether the order accepted Harijans as nuns. At once she asked me whether any other order had invited me to join them. I said yes, while I was working in a convent school earlier, the Sisters had invited me to enter their order. Our Sister said, 'Well, they asked you too, did they? Don't worry about it. You may join us.' I wished I could have disappeared from that spot and vanished then and there. I lamented inwardly that there was no place that was free of caste. And so at last I became a nun and was sent to a convent elsewhere.

I was shocked when I saw this convent and the school attached to it. I couldn't begin to think how I would spend my years in such surroundings. And this convent too was not without its caste divisions. From the very first moment I understood the state of affairs.

In that school, attended by pupils from very wealthy households, people of my community were looking after all the jobs like sweeping the premises, swabbing and washing the classrooms, and cleaning out the lavatories. And in the convent, as well, they spoke very insultingly about low-caste people. They spoke as if they didn't even consider low-caste people as human beings. They did not know that I was a low-caste nun. I was filled with anger towards them, yet I did not have the courage to retort sharply that I too was a low-caste woman. I swallowed the very words that came into my mouth; never said anything out aloud but battled within myself.

According to their notions, low-caste people are all degraded in every way. They think we have no moral discipline nor cleanliness nor culture. They think that this can never be changed. To aid us is like aiding cobras. They speak such words all the time, without even thinking. And I sat there like a lump of tamarind, listening to all this and dying several deaths within. I would tremble to think how they would react if they realized that I was a Dalit. And being a coward, I survived somehow.

In spite of my being a Tamil woman, I was held in some respect because I did all the jobs that were allocated to me capably. But I felt a burning anger when I saw that all the menial jobs there were done by Dalits who were abused all the time and treated in a shameful and degrading way. I was pained to see even older people trembling, shrinking like small children, frightened by the power and wealth that the Sisters had, burying their pride and self-respect, running to do the menial tasks assigned to them. If ever I told them that there was no need for them to die of fear, they need only do their work well, collect their wages and go their way, they would reply that it was all very well for me to say that. After all I was here today, tomorrow I might be somewhere else; it was they who had to stay and suffer. And that struck me as true, too.

* * * *

In this society, if you are born into a low caste, you are forced to live a life of humiliation and degradation until your death. Even after death, caste-difference does not disappear. Wherever you look, however much you study, whatever you take up, caste discrimination stalks us in every nook and corner and drives us into a frenzy. It is because of this that we are unable to find a way to study well and progress like everyone else. And this is why a wretched lifestyle is all that is left to us.

If you are born into a low caste, every moment of your life is a moment of struggle. People screw up their faces and look at us with disgust the moment they know our caste. It is impossible to describe the anguish that look causes. But along with the anguish, there is anger, too. What can our anger do to them, though? It seems we have to swallow our anger and just carry on with our troubled lives.

How did the upper castes become so elevated? How is it that we have been denigrated? They possess money; we do not. If we were wealthy too, wouldn't we learn more, and make more progress than they do? But when it comes to it, even if we are as good as they are, or even better, because of this one issue of caste alone, we are forced to suffer pain and humiliation.

How is it that people consider us too gross even to sit next to when travelling? They look at us with the same look they would cast on someone suffering from a repulsive disease. Wherever we go we suffer blows. And pain. Is there never to be any relief? It doesn't seem to matter whether people are educated or not. They all go about filled with caste hatred. Why, even the nuns and priests, who claim that their hearts are set upon service to God, certainly discriminate according to caste. And in my heart I have even grieved over the fact that I was born as I am.

Are Dalits not human beings? Do they not have common sense? Do they not have such attributes as a sense of honour and self-respect? Are they without any wisdom, beauty, dignity? What do we lack? They treat us in whatever way they choose, as if we are slaves who don't even possess human dignity. And if ever a Dalit gets wise to this and wants to live with some honour and self-respect, they jump up and down as if something really outrageous is happening. They seem to conspire to keep us in our place: to think that we who have worked throughout history like beasts, should live and die like that; we should never move on or go forward.

Because Dalits have been enslaved for generation upon generation, and been told again and again of their degradation, they have come to believe that they are degraded, lacking honour and self-worth, untouchable; they have reached a stage where they themselves, voluntarily, hold themselves apart. This is the worst injustice. This is what even little babies are told, how they are instructed. The consequence of all this is that there is no way for Dalits to find freedom or redemption.

We who are asleep must open our eyes and look about us. We must not accept the injustice of our enslavement by telling ourselves it is our fate, as if we have no true feelings; we must dare to stand up for change. We must crush all these institutions that use caste to bully us into submission, and demonstrate that among human beings there are none who are high or low. Those who have found their happiness by exploiting us are not going to let us go easily. It is we who have to place them where they belong and bring about a changed and just society where all are equal.

Three

I was eleven years old. My mother delivered twin babies; I remember it well. Although we were delighted that a younger brother and sister were born together, it was obvious that the older folk were troubled. They seemed to think that it would be difficult to bring up twins. I really was not old enough to understand it all. It was during this time too that there were frequent disputes between our caste people and the Chaaliyar community. Sometimes these would even develop into full-scale fights.

The cemetery where the Christians buried their dead was just next to the Chaaliyar community school. Only we Dalits buried our dead there, though. The upper-caste Christians had their own cemetery elsewhere. It lay beyond the bus stand. Fights arose between the two castes because the Chaaliyar claimed that our cemetery actually belonged to them. Those Chaaliyar fellows had planned that if they could claim the cemetery by provoking a fight if need be, then it could become part of the playground or gardens of their school. So there were constant fisticuffs and skirmishes between our two communities.

Going by the way people spoke, the Chaaliyar lads didn't have much common sense or wit. They'd wet themselves even if one raised one's voice to them. That was the extent of their courage and daring. But apparently they had much more by way of land, property, and money than we did. It was because of their possessions that they were so uppity. Besides, other caste fellows had spurred them on by jeering at them for being scared of the Parayar. So, even though they knew about the courage and strength of our boys, the Chaaliyar kept on picking quarrels.

Our people forbade the children who normally went past the Chaaliyar settlement on their way to school to walk together in that direction. They cautioned any group who went past that place on their way to the bus stand or the fields to be vigilant. Besides this, they said that women and children should never go there on their own, and that the men should always carry a weapon at their waist while going there or returning from that spot. In spite of all these warnings, one evening there was an outcry that the Chaaliyar had stabbed Izhava's husband, who was from our North Street. Our entire settlement was in shock, people running about here and there, lamenting and shrieking.

I was just coming home from school at the time. My heart began to beat fast when I saw everyone running along the streets, the women hitting themselves on their heads and weeping. But I couldn't understand what it was all about. My mother and grandmother told us we were not to go out of the house. From the doorsteps of our house we could see nothing. At last my grandmother went out to find out what was going on.

'Such a stout man, that Izhava's husband. Yet those Chaaliyar boys stabbed and felled him.'

'It seems that the spear with which they struck his thigh pierced it right through and came out the other side.'

'It seems there was blood everywhere. It seems the old fellow just sank down right there. By a lucky chance that Paniyaaramuttu-Maama saw him at that moment and rushed to tell the menfolk. Otherwise he would have lost the little thread of life left in him.'

'At once they yoked a cart and took him away to the Free Hospital. If he survives, it will be as if he has been granted a new life.'

People were saying things like this in the street.

The men who were standing about in the street were beside themselves with fury. Maama Paralokam spoke up with a frenzied show of heroics, 'What sort of low-down louts these are! It's shameful that men of their sort should come and strike down our fellows. Chi, it's a disgrace, it stinks. Never in history has it been known for a Paraya to die at the hands of a Chaaliyar.' And he spat out his betel juice in a stream.

'If they had the least little bit of decency or manhood, they would have come and fought us face to face. But these are like cowardly women, catching hold of a fellow who was just going about his business, and finishing him off.'

'If you are truly men of our caste, you'll kill ten men in place of the one they took, and garland them with their guts. It's the only way to bring down their pride.'

Even as the old woman, Thavasi, was saying these words, people thudded past us, running towards the cemetery with knives and staves. All the men and women began to run in that direction, then. Behind them, the children followed, weeping with terror. And all the street dogs ran too, barking as they went. The entire street emptied and looked desolate. Only two or three old folk were left at the madatthu saavadi, our caste community hall.

The fighting really came to a head at the cemetery gardens, it seems. All the Chaaliyar women had hidden themselves behind the trees, from where they flung stones and rocks with as much skill as their men might have done. As our men fell behind, the Chaaliyar men ran past them without even pausing to turn around, scrambled into the school building, and locked the doors behind them.

'Look, if they had only fallen into my hands, I'd have pulverized them!'

'They are cowards who take to their heels at the very sight of our faces. How come they put on such airs! Sons of whores!'

After a good deal of exchange of abuse like this, life gradually returned to normal in our street.

For a few days both sides were quiet. Then, all of a sudden, a fight broke out again because some people from our street had beaten up a Chaaliyar caste fellow. At once, the Chaaliyar lot went and placed a complaint against our community at the police station. It seems they had fabricated an elaborate case, putting in a little of what had happened, but also including a lot that had not.

Varkees complained, 'The day they struck Chinnappan-Macchaan, we should have gone and complained at once. We were fools and idiots then. Now look how they've cooked up a whole case against us when we barely touched that man.'

'It seems the charge is against our entire Paraya community, not just the men who were mixed up in the fight.'

'How can he complain against all of us, da? He can only bring a case against the fellows who actually hit him.'

'They've gone and given a statement that all our men went into the Chaaliyar settlement and vandalized their school, their houses, and their temple. They say we threw stones and broke all the tiles of their roofs. They say we dragged their women out and dis-honoured them, and that we entered their houses and looted their property.'

'Well, but have these policemen gone and lost their brains? Won't they have to hold a proper enquiry?'

'Exactly. Just because a man chooses to say what he likes, does it mean that the fellow who listens has to lose his commonsense? Let the police go and see for themselves whether they can find any damage to those people's houses.'

'It seems they anticipated that, broke some of their own tiled roofs here and there, heaped up some rocks and stones at likely places, and set it all up.'

'So now, what are we going to do?'

'That's it, macchaan. We have to get our headman to organize us, house by house. Then we must collect all the weapons we will need. That boy, Katterumbu's son, he knows how to make country-bombs. We must have some ready. We'll show them. We won't let them off.'

And so, having made a few decisions, they then went away, about their business.

As I heard more and more of this kind of talk, I began to wish desperately that I could see the showdown that had been planned to take place in the cemetery. But I knew that my family would never allow me to go. At the time of the fray they would keep me locked in and never let me go out. The school gave us a holiday, though. And just by chance my younger brother and sister both fell ill. It seemed it was always like that with the twins. Whatever illness they had, they always had it together. My mother took one child, my grandmother the other, and they set off, carrying them, to walk the two miles to the hospital. As they left, they told me to look after the house and see to my other sister. At that time, I was the oldest child among those of us who were at home. After me, there was my seven-year-old sister.

In a short while, the street was in an uproar. I went to the door and stuck my head out. Men and women were running along without stopping, talking about the fight that was going on, at that very moment, at the cemetery. I really wanted to go with them. Now, to go to the cemetery from our house, you had to cross four or five streets and come to the very edge of the village. There was a huge fig tree in the cemetery. I had been there before, to gather the fruit. I had also been there with other children when a threshing floor had been set up and the paddy winnowed.

I desperately wanted to go and watch the fight, but at the same time, I was reluctant too. And I was also afraid that if my mother arrived and found out, I'd be properly thrashed. For some time I hesitated. Then I took courage, told my little sister to look after the house, and rushed off towards the cemetery.

Our people were standing on our side of the street flinging their stones. I saw an uncle of ours standing there along with the rest, throwing stones. Then the men began to move forward, still throwing stones, and carrying sticks and poles, while all the women and children followed, very, very slowly, terrified. From the Chaaliyar settlement side, not a single man was to be seen. Nor were they throwing stones. I thought that they were surely defeated. All the children of my age said the same thing. We told each other gleefully that all the Chaaliyar had run away and hidden, and that we had most certainly won.

Even as we were rejoicing, it all turned into a tragedy. All of a sudden, a huge gang of policemen came out of the Chaaliyar settlement, batons in hand, drove our men back ruthlessly, mercilessly beating up those they caught, before arresting them. We couldn't make out where the police had hidden themselves for so long. All of us fled, fearing for our lives. The men made straight for the fields and woods and tried to hide there. The police chased and caught as many as they could. It seems those of our men who couldn't run any more, just lay down among the crops and held their breath. Then the police came to our part of the village, rounded up all the men whom they found there and beat them black and blue. Still raining blows on them, they drove them into their lorries. A few men escaped by running as fast as they could, along the shores of the lake, and away. And it was they who told the men who were hiding in the fields not to return, but to stay there among the mountains and the woods.

We children and all the women ran as fast as we could, falling over each other, until we stumbled into our houses. Outside, we heard the thud-thud of police boots stamping up and down, the sharp sounds of blows as our men were struck repeatedly, and the yells, 'Ayyo Amma,' of unendurable pain. As the women saw their husbands, their children, their fathers, and their brothers being beaten, they cried out in pity. At that time there were no men in our own household. Both my father and my elder brother were away elsewhere. Yet I too could not help weeping. And my sister wept with me. As we were weeping together, my mother and grandmother returned home from the hospital. Even as they approached, they could see the police beating and arresting our men and they were frightened. Paatti asked me, 'Why, whatever happened, di? Did the fighting break out again?'

I told them all that had happened. They only said, 'Who told you to go to the cemetery and watch the fight? What would we have done if one of those stones had fallen on you and broken your skull?' They let it go at that. Everyone was in such a state of shock that I escaped. Had it been another time, I would have got a good hiding.

The crying and shouting didn't come to an end until evening time. But then, in the evening, the whole street was as silent and still and as desolate as a cremation ground. Not a single man could be seen. Only the women huddled together here and there, whispering among themselves. I couldn't understand anything. At home, we didn't say a word to each other. We sat there, silent. Now and then, if my baby brother or sister cried, I ran to their cradle and rocked it, afraid of their making the slightest noise. In the dense silence of our street, the babies' cries cut into our hearts with a sharp pain. Paatti arrived at night. She explained in detail all that had happened that day.

'It seems that the Chaaliyar folk invited some people known as the "Reserve Police" all the way from Sivakasi, butchered a sheep for them, and arranged a feast. They've taken an oath to destroy our boys, they say, so without counting the cost they are slaughtering sheep at the rate of two a day and feasting the police. Do we have such means? Here we are, struggling just for this watery gruel. So how will the police or the government be on our side?'

'It seems that every single man they could catch sight of they beat up and then arrested.'

'What will they do to them, Paatti?' I asked.

'They'll take them and they'll whip them like they whip animals until they can neither see nor breathe, and then they'll clap them in jail, just barely alive. That's what they say.'

'And Paatti, will they give them food to eat after they have beaten them up?'

'What food? Rubbish! They'll give them a tiny bit of ragi or cholam gruel in the name of food, they say. Now if they were rich, or upper caste, or if the police were obliged to them in some way, they would just have given them a couple of light taps. They would have looked after them well enough.'

'And Paatti, when will they let them go home?'

'They have to survive, first of all. After all those blows, after they have been subject to torture, after the case is adjourned several times, and then heard at last, heaven only knows when they'll come home.'

That night, nobody could sleep. All through the night the police prowled round and round our streets. There was no sound at all, except for the sound of the policemen's boots and the barking of the dogs. The very sound of the boots was frightening. Each step felt as if the boot was treading on my chest and pressing down. I wanted to cry out aloud. But I lay there in fear, my hand pressed to my throat. If any of the young ones started to cry, our women hastened to quieten them in whatever way they could. It was like that in our house too. There was a fear in our hearts that if the police heard the noise, they would come into our houses. Even the slightest noise sounded huge to us, made our insides quake.

The next morning, the women did all their usual work as well as that of the men. The police continued to prowl round and about. It seems they had turned up in order to gather up every single man who had escaped them so far. That morning, very fearfully, I came out and sat on our front verandah-ledge. A number of women were gathered outside, talking together. They spoke in low voices about what had happened the previous day, as if they were exchanging secrets.

'It seems that the police beat up a certain Alphonse very severely in the middle of the street. It seems he couldn't stop vomiting blood. They say it is unlikely he'll survive.'

'In North Street, while they were beating up Maariappa's son, it seems a five rupee note fell out of his pocket. It seems his mother stooped to pick it up, weeping all the time. At once a policeman put his boot against her stomach, kicked her aside, and took the money himself.'

'They caught hold of the teacher who lives on North Street and thrashed him soundly. He bowed to them with folded hands and pleaded, saying, "Saar, I'm only a teacher, saar. I don't stick my head into all these things, saar." They gave him another couple of blows, but left him alone after that.'

As they were saying all this to each other, we heard the sound of boots approach, and everyone ran away. I too went in hastily, and locked the door.

As usual, the women went to the fields where they worked as day-labourers. On their way, they took gruel to the men hiding in the woods, told them the news, and went on. And so the women somehow managed on their own, even without their men's earnings. Every day the police walked around the streets. Then they began to enter the houses one by one, in search of the men who were in hiding. It seems the Pallar men had tipped off the police that some of our men might actually be hiding inside their houses. When Paatti heard this she was furious. She railed against them in a single breath. 'Look at these Palla boys; they'll betray their own people. When these boys were terrified of the police and hiding from them, all of them lay safely in Paraya houses. They ate our food and drank our water. We took them in and protected them because we believed they were our people. Now, look, they can't feel the same about us.'

At that very moment, someone banged on our door violently. While all the rest of us were cowering with fear, certain that it must be the police, my grandmother went and opened the door. The headman leapt inside, dashed into the big earthenware enclosure where we stored paddy, and hid himself there. His mother followed him in and said, 'The police are searching even now, from house to house. He can't run and hide anywhere else at this time. There are police surrounding the whole area. Please hide him somehow; please protect him.' Then she went and sat down, outside. We were all terrified. I thought to myself, please God, please don't let the police come to our house.

We continued to hear the thuds as the police struck their heavy blows, our men screaming in pain, and women shouting and yelling in protest. We trembled within as we heard all this. I stood on the ledge-like bench within the house and looked out, and I could see the steel helmets of the police going past our house, in rows. In the next few minutes, ten or twelve of them had marched their way right inside. My mother stood stock still, one of the babies in her arms. They kicked open every door and looked inside all the rooms. They peeped into the bathing area. They glanced over the place where the firewood was stacked.

The naataamai, having dashed into the room where the storage jar was kept, had shut its half doors, bolted them from the inside, and retreated well within the jar. The police kicked at the half-doors, and when they wouldn't open, summoned my mother and ordered her to open them. When my mother tried to shift them, it became apparent that they were locked on the inside. Now the police were suspicious. They accused my mother of hiding people there and acting out some sort of charade. Then they kicked the doors open, breaking them apart, burst in, caught hold of the man who was hiding there in the jar, lifted him out by his hair, and rained blows upon him. Tears filled my eyes. This was the first time that I had ever seen the police beating up a person they had seized. If one policeman slapped the headman's face, all the rest followed, slapping him in the very same spot. If one stamped on him, then everyone else did the same. At last, still hitting him, they dragged him to the door and kicked him outside. His mother, who was outside, pleaded and wept saying, 'Ayya, he is the headman of this place. Leave him alone, saami.' In reply they said, 'Oh, so he's the headman, is he?' And they gave him a few more blows.

In spite of all these atrocities, it turned out that in two or three houses, the women managed to hide their men and save them. In one house, they shut up the man inside, and sent the police away, saying, 'Ayya, she's just started her labour pains; there's no one else here.' It was all dark inside the house. The police believed the story and went away.

In another house, a woman thrust her husband inside a sack and sat on top of it, saying, 'Ayya, I've got a cold and fever. It's four days since my husband went away; he hasn't been in these parts at all, saami.' And so the police left.

Then right at the middle of the street, they hid two men and said, 'Ayya, our little girl is covered in small pox. Please don't go in with your boots on. There's nobody else here, Ayya.' The police, apparently, didn't even enter the house when they heard this. It seems the police behaved deplorably towards the women as they went from house to house. They used obscene language and swore at them, told them that since their husbands were away they should be ready to entertain the police at night, winked at them, and shoved their guns against their bodies.

From sunset time the women began to be scared out of their minds. While there was still a little light they cooked and ate some gruel, then they gathered the children together, and went off to sleep in the church courtyard. Some women even untied their cows and calves and took them along. Not a fly nor a cow was to seen on the streets. When I saw what was happening, I too was frightened. I went up to my mother and tried to persuade her that we too should go away to the church. But she asked me, how was she to manage in the church with two tiny babies? Where would she tie up the two cradles for the twins? So she refused to go. In the end we were the only folk to stay at home that night.

And at night, the police again walked round and round. But they didn't enter our house. In the morning, the women returned to the street as usual, and set off for their customary coolie work. The police were furious that the women were smart enough to continue working and taking care of their children even without their men, and so they rounded up all the women workers, forced them into their lorries, and dropped them off on the other side, in the village. The police were really riled when they heard that the women who went to work were actually taking food to the men who were hiding in the forest.

Then two or three days later, someone informed the police that some men were hiding in the church, just beneath the belfry. At once they came in a posse, climbed up to the belfry, grabbed all those whom they found there, and dragged them bodily through the Chaaliyar street.

The women said it was our local parish priest who had informed the police. All the same, one of the men who had hidden in the church escaped somehow and the police went after him. At that time, a man from another caste was ploughing the priest's fields. The man who escaped grabbed the plough from the other man's hand, sent him away, and daubed himself all over with the wet earth. Then he drove the bullocks, did not show his face directly to the police, and got by that way. But in spite of all these strategies and hardships, about three-quarters of the total male population of our community were caught at last. A few had disappeared into the mountain jungle.

The case was heard at court. We were told that all the men had been moved to the Marudai jail. There was no money to pay for the hearing. So the women divided the cost among themselves and arranged to collect the money.

Now just at that time, a small boy died. He was just ten years old, from a family living on the North Street. They were distantly related to us. We were frightened even to go near the cemetery. The Chaaliyar boys used to hang around there. In our streets, constantly patrolled by the police, there was no other male presence. Everyone was in a quandary about what to do with the boy's body at a time like this. Then there was the other anxiety that before he was buried, his father should at least see him. At last my Paatti and some of the older women sat together, talked, and made a plan.

They decided that two women would go to the mandavam fields where the boy's father was hiding. They would take a sari with them when they went. They would find him and fetch him home in the darkness of the night. They'd make him wear the sari, disguise himself as a woman, cover his head, and pretend to be a mourner attending the funeral. At the same time that evening, some others would go to the cemetery and prepare a grave for the burial.

Apparently one woman asked what they should do if there was any trouble while they were digging the grave. At once my Paatti had said, 'Go away you crazy thing, you know that these Chaaliyar boys take a couple of policemen with battery operated torches to watch over them even when they relieve themselves. If we go together at evening time and stand together, they won't come out, even to shit. All their song and dance display is because these policemen protect them. Anyway even the police will never go near the cemetery once daylight's gone. They'll tuck into their free fodder and then stretch themselves out to sleep.'

Now, the mandavam fields lay about four or five miles to the north of us. Near the mandavam there was a banyan tree. People said a fire-breathing pisaasu lived in the branches of that tree, keeping guard over seven cauldrons of coins. It would try to lure passers-by, showing them the coins out of a cauldron. They said that countless people had seen that pisaasu. They said it stood very tall, between the sky and the earth. Its hair hung in long matted locks. Each nail had grown as long and sharp as a knife. Its eyes glowed like torches. Smoke streamed out of its mouth and nostrils. Also it could appear in any form it chose. Some people had seen it as a tiny baby, some as a fox, and some even as a young girl. And it was towards this very same mandavam that the women were hurrying with their sari.

Meantime, some others took their shovels to the cemetery after the sun went down, and began to dig the grave. At the dead of night, between ten and twelve, the father came disguised in a sari, saw his son, and stood silent, stunned, unable even to cry out loud. On their way home, they had been stopped by the police. The accompanying women had immediately raised a funeral dirge, an oppaari, wept aloud and said, 'The sad news has just reached us, saami. We come from the next village to attend the funeral.' The police had moved them on.

They kept a vigil all night, and even before cock-crow the women set out with the dead body and buried him themselves, in the cemetery. Before dawn broke properly, the boy's father set off in his sari with the two women accompanying him some distance; then, he disappeared into the same mandavam fields. Everyone talked about this incident in our parts the next day. Everyone was full of praise; they said how clever the women had been and how smartly they had managed everything themselves.

A few days later, some of the men who had been taken away and arrested were returned on bail. Others were still kept imprisoned. The case went on for a long time, with repeated adjournments. In the midst of all this, Middle Street Alphonse, who had been beaten by the police until he vomited blood, died the second day after he was let out of jail. They wept as they buried him, saying, 'He was such a robust man. But with the thrashing the police gave him, he went, just like that.'

Little by little, we began to forget the fighting over the cemetery. The Paraya community and the Chaaliyar community began to act towards each other in a normal way once again. The older women of the Chaaliyar community came into our streets to gather cowdung, or to sell gram and fried tamarind seeds.

Suddenly one day, as I was coming home from school, I saw everyone running towards the bus stand. By this time I had moved on to a different class in school. When I asked what was going on, people said that the cemetery case had gone in our favour, and that all our men were released and were coming home. I went straight home, flung my school bag down, and went racing with the other children to watch the fun. And, yes, all the men of our street came home. As the husbands came home, each was asked to step over a long-handed pestle used for pounding grain, which was laid across the front entrance of the house. After that they were given water to bathe. Then they were handed new veshtis and shoulder cloths to put on, and taken indoors at last. They did this in every house where the men returned. Everywhere there was laughter.

'We have been burying our dead in this cemetery since my grandfather's time at least. Now suddenly these fellows turned up with their bullying tactics. God himself wouldn't stand for it. That's why we won the case.'

'It's that St Anthony who brought us victory.'

'They thought our Paraya boys would be easy game. But Our Lady exposed that thought for the sham it is, didn't she?'

'We must have a sung Mass, a Pusai, in gratitude next Sunday.'

'Why must there be a Pusai sung, di? Did this priest ever help us, even with the dust of his feet? When our men who were hiding in the church were caught and taken away, this priest was sitting at ease in his bungalow, one leg slung over the other, smoking his cigarette happily and watching it all.'

'And not only that, sister-in-law. We didn't have the money to attend the adjournment and asked the priest for a paltry loan of a few rupees, but he refused outright.'

Bama 45

People talked in this way, taking different sides. But in the end, there was just great happiness that the case turned out in our favour.

* * * *

After this particular inter-caste trouble, there were also skirmishes between the Pallar and the Parayar on many occasions. Every time there would be just a small altercation that flared up into a terrible fight between the two communities.

The first fight between the Pallar and the Parayar was all because of a ripe banana. A man from the Palla street, known as Ondiviran, was coming along, his cart loaded with a bunch of bananas. The young lad, Pavulu, grandson of Thavasi-Pethiya, went and pulled off two or three of the fruit and ate them. The very first words between the two were abusive, and the verbal abuse very soon turned into a fist-fight. Then four other Palla boys joined in and beat up Pavulu, raining blows upon him. Just as Pavulu came home to our area and complained about what had happened, several Pallars entered the Paraya quarter with their sticks and knives. Just then there were not so many men in the Paraya quarter. Two or three old men, a few young boys, and Susai who was on leave from the army, joined together, and went with folded hands to try and make peace. Even though the stone-throwing continued, somehow they dared to press on and say to them, 'Appa, should we come to blows and actually kill each other over a mere banana? Let us call a village meeting and settle things peacefully.' But they had a real struggle on their hands before they could get the others to agree. Anyhow, they finally managed to call a meeting, and to punish Pavulu appropriately.

After this particular fight, the boys on both sides nursed their vengeance. Four or five months later a fight erupted in the ration shop. That effeminate grandson of Benjamin's went and made trouble in the ration shop, and another fight flared up between the Parayar and the Pallar. This time neither side would give in, and they challenged and fought each with everything they had. The Palla boys stood at the edge of the lake and flung stones. The Parayar threw stones in retaliation, and it really turned into a pitched battle. Some of the more daring women from the Paraya community took idli steamer lids to fend off the stones that were aimed at them, and joined in the fray.

While this fight was going on, the military man, Susai, ran as fast as his heels could carry him along the fields to report it to the police station. On the way he saw four or five Pallars with sickles in their hands, parading along the shore. By some kind saint's favour, he turned suddenly, and on the pretext of washing his hands and feet, climbed into the well of the Kaakkaa-mandai and hid there. Otherwise they might have caught him and chopped him up then and there. As soon as their heads were hidden, he raced along the ridge of the fields and brought back the police with him. And as soon as the police arrived, the men fled like a flock of crows.

So for some time there was an uneasy kind of peace. But a few days later, as Monangi's son was standing at the oil shop, buying something, a number of Palla boys joined together and beat him up. When the boy came running home half dead to tell us what had happened, a real brawl followed.

Just when it seemed that the hostilities were abating a bit, a few Pallars caught hold of a Paraya boy who had gone into the woods, hacked him anyhow, and buried him then and there. The Paraya men went and dug up his body and removed it to the cemetery. After that, they watched out for a hapless Palla boy who had gone eastward to graze his goats, fell upon him and killed him. After that the police came, dragged away the boys from both castes to the police station, shoved them in jail, and locked them up.

The case still goes on. Adjournments upon adjournment follow each other. Because of the case, the boys on both sides cover their backsides, and go about circumspectly. God knows what will happen in the end. They fight to the death one moment; the next moment they join together again. Suddenly, and for no reason at all they'll be fighting and wrestling with each other. A hundred times a second there are scuffles amongst them. Shameless fellows. Of course the upper-caste men will laugh at them. Instead of uniting together in a village of many castes, if they keep challenging each other to fights, what will happen to all these men in the end?

Four

From the time I was a small child, I saw people working hard; I grew up amongst such people. At home, my mother and my grandmother laboured from sunrise to sunset, without any rest. And to this day, in my village, both men and women can survive only though hard and incessant labour.

There is work of various kinds. If you look at agricultural labour, there's ploughing, manuring, watering, sowing the seed, separating the seedlings and planting them out; then, weeding, spraying the fields with fertilizer, reaping the grain, working on the threshing floors, planting groundnut, selecting ripe coconuts. All this. Apart from this work in the fields, there's construction labour: digging wells, carrying loads of earth, gravel, and stone. If even this is not available, then people have to go up to the hills to gather firewood, or they must work with palm-leaves, or at the kilns making bricks. People have to do some work in order to eat.

More than three-quarters of the land in these parts are in the hands of the Naickers. People of our community work for them, each Paraya family attached to a Naicker family, as pannaiyaal, bonded labourers. As far as I have seen, it is only Palla and Paraya communities who work in this way. Other communities don't have to work so hard.

The Koravar or gypsies, and leather-working Chakkiliyar would sweep the streets, dredge and clean the drains, and make a living that way. Sometimes they wove winnowing trays, boxes, baskets for carrying paddy, and chicken coops, and earned a few coins that way. Everyone in my community had to work hard for their livelihood. Only a few of the teachers' families lived in any degree of comfort.

Everybody said that my Paatti was a true and proper servant. She worked as a labourer to a Naicker family, but she was also a Kotthaal—she hired labourers for them, brought them to work regularly, supervised them, and made sure they received their wages. Except for Sundays, she went to work every single day. Sometimes, if the Naicker insisted, she would rush through Pusai before daylight on Sunday, and then run to work. She'd rise before cock-crow at two or three in the morning, draw water, see to the household chores, walk a long distance to the Naicker's house, work till sunset, and then come home in the dark and cook a little gruel for herself.

When I was a bit older, Paatti used to take me to the fields with her. We were not a household with many comforts or conveniences. During the school term, as soon as lessons were over, I'd go and collect such things as the thorns used for fences, or palmyra and coconut-palm stems and fronds for fuel. I would collect fresh cowdung and pat it into flat cakes for burning. Sometimes I would go into the fields and pick up dried cowdung.

During the school holidays, I would go with Paatti or some other woman to work in the fields. Most often I helped to pull up the groundnut crop and to clean and sort the pods. Small children were not asked to do anything harder than this.

To pull up the groundnut crop and to clean and separate the pods, you had to wake up very early, well before cock-crow, pour some millet porridge into a carrying vessel, and run with it. In the fields, you had to pull up a heap of groundnut plants, and then sit down to pulling off the pods. At midday break, we would drink our kuuzh along with a mouthful of fresh nuts. We would separate and clean the pods until sunset time, and then carry them to the Naicker's granaries. There, the Naicker's pannaiyaal would measure the cleaned groundnuts by the marakkaal, and pay us five or ten paise for each marakkaal. However hard we pushed ourselves, it never came to more than five rupees in all. We'd take what we were given, and come home only at dusk. After we came home, we'd buy a little rice, light the hearth, and cook some gruel.

If we were going to glean the last of the groundnut crop that was left over in the fields, we would go somewhat later. We'd go here and there all over the fields where the groundnut crop had been pulled up, and use our shovels at random to hammer into the earth and rake it, so that we could pick up all the stray groundnuts. The Naickers were never happy about this, though. They would chase us, throw stones and pieces of wood at us, and drive us away. Occasionally, some of the Naickers would allow us to glean and strip the fields on condition that we gave them half or a third of what we had found. If we found any groundnuts, well and good. If not, we had nothing. In any case, the Naickers would only let us go home in the evening, after they had taken their share. We would take what was left to the chekkadi, the bazaar where the oil-press was at one time, sell it to the tradesmen there and buy some rice or a little broken grain. You couldn't put the broken-grain gruel in your mouth. It stank so much. But if we had no money, broken-grain gruel was all we could eat. Sometimes I sold my groundnuts and brought the money home to my mother. Sometimes, I just gave her the groundnuts.

We'd go at daybreak to the Naicker's house to shell the groundnuts. Here they would measure out the dried groundnuts to us, by the marakkaal. We'd sit in the cattle shed, take up the groundnuts in both hands alternately, and break the shells by smashing them against the floor. If we were in a great hurry, we'd use both hands as well as our teeth to shell the groundnuts. If you used your teeth, your mouth would fill with dust and your throat would choke. But could one afford to bother about all that? We had to work as hard as we could to shell all the nuts. At the same time we had to be careful not to crack the nuts themselves. If too many of the nuts were broken, the Naicker would be really angry. You can't use broken nuts as seeds, can you? That's why. If we chatted in between shelling, or ate one or two of the nuts, that was it. The Naicker would be furious and swear at us, using every term of abuse he knew. They paid us five to ten paisa per marakkaal. So we didn't make that much money this way either. At the very most, we'd make five or six rupees. Even so, I went with Paatti to shell groundnuts.

If none of this work was available, I'd go off to collect stray onions left in the field or thorny twigs. Some days I'd go with other children to collect firewood from the mountain jungle. On such days, I'd wake up in the early morning, pour some kuuzh into a carrier, and collect four annas from my mother to give to the 'Guarder' or forester. If we didn't give any money to the Guarder he would not allow us to collect any firewood. He lived in the forestry bungalow and had a habit of coming round on inspection unexpectedly.

It wasn't that easy to go into the jungle. We had to climb the steep mountain slopes one by one, pick up the dried pieces of wood that lay here and there, and then tie them together into bundles. Before you could manage to do this, the twigs and thorns would scratch and tear your face, your hair, your arms and legs. Sometimes your skin would be all torn and bleeding. But if you worried about all this, there was no way you could gather firewood. Sometimes your hair would get all entangled in the branches and nearly split your skull apart. You never knew which way to go forward. What roads or paths were there for you to take? We had to push and shove and crawl our way through bushes and briars.

After all this struggle and hardship, you couldn't just tie up your bundle, lift it on to your head and walk home. Something would pull you back here, a tree or a creeper would block your way there. So you could never climb down the hill easily. You had to creep along gradually, slowly rolling the firewood bundle forward. Having reached the base of the hill one way or another, you could then carry your bundle on your head and walk home, by which time, what little energy that was left in you would have ebbed away, and the load would feel really heavy. It wasn't a short distance, after all, between the mountain jungle and our village. The others would bring their bundles to the Naicker street and sell them for seven or eight rupees each. But I never actually sold a bundle of firewood. I took mine home for our use.

In those days, my mother too used to go collecting firewood. On one occasion she brought home a bundle of firewood, leaned it against the wall, and then began vomiting vast gobs of blood. But it was only by toiling like this, without taking any account of their bodies as human flesh and blood, that people of my community could even survive. As soon as children grew up to be ten or twelve years of age, they'd go and find some way of making money. Until that time, they'd go about carrying their younger siblings on their hips. They'd even gather a few twigs and sticks, and learn to boil a little gruel. It was always the girl children who had to look after all the chores at home. The older women would come home in the evenings after a day's work, and then see to the household jobs. If there were boys in the house, they would graze the sheep and cattle. When they grew a bit older, they'd go off to work in the fields like the older men.

When it was harvest time, we used to take a wide winnowing tray and stiff broom, and go and stand by the lake shore or even by the bank of the filthy canal, so that we could sweep and gather up the ears of grain falling off the sheaves that were being carried to the threshing floor. We'd winnow the grain we collected and take it home. But it was only the young children and the old women who did this. Grown-up girls and women in their prime, though, went directly to the fields, winnowed the grain there by the basketful and were paid in kind.

In this way, whatever we made, either by picking up the scattered grain with great difficulty, or from winnowing it in the fields, we then took to the shops. There were Nadar men who would set up shop in our streets, weigh the grain, and take it in exchange for tapioca or some such other goods. And at that time, we never realized how badly we were swindled during these bartering sessions.

In exactly the same way, when the cotton pods burst, we'd bring the cotton we gathered, and exchange it for goods. The tradesmen always managed to collect several bundles of cotton or grain for themselves by cheating us. Our hard work was exploited half the time by our Naicker employers. The rest of the time we were swindled by these tradesmen. So how was it possible for us to make any progress? It seems that it is only the swindlers who manage to advance themselves. But there is no way at all for the Dalit who sticks to fair methods, and who toils hard all her life, to make good.

Until the time that I was in the eighth class, I worked in my village in all these ways. All the time I went to work for the Naickers, I knew I should not touch their goods or chattels; I should never come close to where they were. I should always stand away to one side. These were their rules. I often felt pained and ashamed. But there was nothing that I could do. They belonged to a higher caste. They had the money. We had to listen to what they said. However furious or resentful I felt in my heart, I have stepped aside for them, along with the other women of my community.

I was admitted into the convent school in the nearby village so that I could attend the ninth class. There I did not have to work all the time like this. I ate my meals, and I studied; that was all. During the holidays I returned to my own village. Children who boarded at the convent and studied there certainly had a special status in our village. All the same, when I went home I did all the chores that fell to me customarily.

After the tenth class, I finished my final exams and went home. My mother was walking from the street of the Naickers with a bundle on her head, made up of mango wood which she had gathered and tied together. I went along with her, back and forth, with two or three head loads of firewood which I gathered for her. To come to our part of village from the Naicker street, you had to cross the Nadar street, the Thevar street, and then come past the oil-press and bazaar. Some people who had seen me carrying the firewood said to my mother with astonishment, 'Your daughter has finished her schooling at the convent, yet she doesn't mind carrying firewood like this.' I don't know why they were so surprised. In those days I really enjoyed that kind of hard physical labour. It is only recently that I find I cannot do it any more. Because I've been to other places and have been engaged in studying different things, I find that my body isn't as flexible as it used to be.

When I saw our people working so hard night and day, I often used to wonder from where they got their strength. And I used to think, that at the rate they worked, men and women both, every single day, they should really be able to advance themselves. But of course, they never received a payment that was appropriate to their labour. And another thing. Even if they did the same work, men received one wage, women another. They always paid men more. I could never understand why.

Even though they worked so hard and suffered bodily pain, our people laughed and were cheerful. This is a community that was born to work. And however hard they toil, it is the same kuuzh every day. The same broken-grain gruel. The same watery dried-fish curry. It seems they never ever reflect upon their own terrible state of affairs. But do they have any time to think? You have to wonder how the upper castes would survive without these people. For it's only when they fall asleep at night that their arms and legs are still; they seem to be at work at all other times. And they have to keep working until the moment of death. It is only in this way that they can even half fill their bellies.

Mind you, things get steadily worse and worse. In the old days, it is true, even tiny tots would hold on to sheep and cattle, and look after babies as they tumbled about in the streets around their houses. Nowadays, poor things, they go to work like adults. At crack of dawn, even before the Madurai bus makes its appearance, these days the van from the matchbox factory will arrive. These tiny, crab-like children pour their kuuzh into their carriers half asleep, totter along to the van, climb in and go off to work. They work at sticking on matchbox labels; they make firecrackers and use chemicals; and they return home exhausted, at seven in the evening. At an age when they should be going to school, studying like everyone else and playing about in the evenings, they are shut up inside the factories instead. There are two or three schools available for the children nowadays. But these little ones' fate is the smell of matchbox solution, not the smell of knowledge or learning. How can they afford to study, when it is such a struggle even to fill their bellies?

Five

There was nothing special that was laid on for us by way of recreation or pastimes in our streets. When school was over, we children joined together and played our games; that was all. We made no distinction between boys and girls. We played together, as if we were all the same.

There were a few games that we played most frequently. Two or three boys would play at being Naicker. The rest of us would call them, 'Ayya, Ayya', and pretend to be their pannaiyaal. These boys would act as if they had a lot of power over us. They'd call out to us, 'Yeppa, Yeppa', humiliate us, and make us do a lot of work. We'd pretend to work in the fields all day, and then collect our wages and go home.

We also played at keeping shop. The boys managed the shops, pretending to be the Nadar Mudalaali. We'd go there, hand over our tile-money and buy all sorts of groceries to take home. 'Tile-money' was made of broken shards of mud-pots which we shaped into round pieces.

Sometimes we'd go to the lake and bring some clay which we shaped into pots and pans and dolls to play with. There were other good games too. We'd play at giving circus shows, or kuuthu performances;

sometimes we danced or did a kummi. Sometimes we played at being nuns and priests who came and gave us blows.

Then we played at being married and setting off on a bus journey; the husband coming home drunk and hitting his wife; the police arriving and beating him up.

But these were the games that we played only as very small children. As we grew a little older, then the games changed accordingly. As older children, we went together to the lake or the well to catch fish. Sometimes we went with the boys to collect the wild manjanatthi and kodukka fruit which they threw down from the trees; we ate the fruit they gave us; we wandered about with them. Then the older girls would play dice games, or hop and catch, or other indoor games with tamarind seeds and pebbles, and board games like pallaanguzhi, and thattaangal. The boys too had their own games: catching games, games with sticks, spinning tops, marbles.

And then we played kabaddi as well. After we returned from the church in the evening, sometimes we played late into the night before going home to sleep. Those who had baby brothers and sisters would lull them to sleep on their shoulders and join in the game of carrying petromax lamps in procession. We'd make toy chariots out of dried maize sticks and carry them around in procession, a few of us walking ahead, the others following on with the petromax lamps. We used to make drums out of cattle-membrane and skin, and bang them as we went along. It used to be such fun. We marched along, street by street. At last we'd come back to the shrine of St Sebastian and put down the chariot there. You should have watched the fun as we went past our own houses. We'd each have a sly smirk on our faces then. Some of the older people would laugh at us and tease us. Others would follow us, ranting and raving away. Of course it was to be expected they'd scold us, when we went through the entire street, shouting and banging like that.

Children from other communities would walk along the lake shore, all dolled up, on their way to the cinema. But the rules of the village ensured that none of the women from our community went to the cinema. They said that this was because the boys of all the other communities would pull our women about if they were seen in the cinema hall. Then there would be fights all around. So, anyway, only our men went. And mostly it was only the younger fellows who went to the cinema.

When we girls grew up, there was no more play. We went to work during the day, came home and saw to the household chores; that was it. There was nothing else. Now even the little ones don't play any more. Even the tiny ones wake up at cock-crow, go to the matchbox factory, and work there till sunset.

As if the idea had suddenly hit them, the men of the village would play at silambam. For this, they had long staffs with which they would fence. I didn't understand anything about it. All the same, when silambam matches took place in front of the community hall, I'd be the first person to go and stand there as a spectator. In the same way, the young men would also get together for a kabaddi game. That used to be really exciting. Lots of people from our street would go and watch. The men sometimes played cards, sitting under the trees. They gambled for money, and sometimes came to blows. But if the police turned up suddenly, they'd run for it, not even caring if their veshtis fell off, and vanish from sight.

Near the community hall, there was a great ball-like stone. People called it the youth stone. It seems that in the evenings, young men would lift it high into the air and throw it down to the ground. It seems it was a way of demonstrating their strength.

In the old days, there used to be jalli-kattu or bull chasing during the Pongal season. Now it's been banned. Nobody runs a jalli-kattu any more. At Christmas and Easter times there would be kabaddi matches in the village. Sometimes the match would be between teams of boys, all of whom were from our streets. Otherwise it would be between our boys and the boys from the next village. There would be crowds bustling about at such times.

Apart from all this, on Christmas and Easter days, they would set up 'radios' and 'mike sets'. It was only much later that I realized that what we were calling 'radios' were actually loudspeakers. In those days, nobody in our village had this kind of equipment. They used to have to borrow it all from the next village.

As soon as the man with the mike set arrived at our bus stand, that was it! All the small children ran to the bus stand, and accompanied him back to our streets. Our boys would help by carrying the 'radio' themselves. Even as they came along, they would put their mouths to the speaker and say Hello, Hello, and suchlike. I too longed to touch it as the boys did, to try speaking into it. But I never once got the chance to do it.

After they had brought the equipment and set it up, the first thing they did was to play the song, *Ask and ye shall receive; knock and it shall be opened unto you; seek and ye shall find.* As soon as they heard the sound, all the little children from the houses nearby would come running up to the raised dais like little mice. We'd show our happiness by racing up the steps and jumping down from there. If we were in a state of high excitement, we'd push each other off on to the ground, fall on top of each other, roll about, and get up in delight.

After a while, we'd go home to put on our new clothes, slick down our hair with oil, plait it and put flowers in it, spit into the hard pottu-powder, scrape it together to make a paste to dot the forehead, and then return to the dais in the community hall. Now we'd finger each other's new clothes in turn and talk endlessly about them, sharing our happiness.

If this was the case among the little ones, the older girls went about laughing amongst themselves in their own way. You could make out their joy even in the way they drew the water from the well opposite the hall, in their firm tread, water pots at their hips. During those days, the entire street would be bustling with joy.

As for the lads, they put on their new trousers, flapping loose in some cases, skin-tight in others; slicked down their hair in all kinds of styles, and walked about touching their hair now and then and smiling in a certain way. Some boys would wear shining white veshtis down to their feet, and long shirts over red banians. Everywhere you could see different colours.

On feast days, they would build canopies in front of the shrines in the street, with banana trees tied to either side. We'd hold on to the canopy posts and twirl about in play. Sometimes the posts would shake and come loose when we did this. Women would come to place lighted candles at the shrines and to worship. Those candles were actually quite handy for small boys to light their bidis. They'd pick up the bidi stubs that old men had thrown away, light them up, and smoke in secret. Sometimes, we girls would watch for fun. But if there was an argument, we'd threaten to tell their mothers that we'd seen them smoke bidi stubs.

As soon as the mike set arrived in the village, the boys would want to speak into it as they pleased, one after another. They'd sing songs. Some others would beat out the rhythm appropriately. They'd call out to each other, loudly, to come and sing. Sometimes it would all end in a wrangle.

In the past, there used to be a man in our parts, called Uudan, blower. I don't know what his real name was. There wasn't a single person in the village who didn't know him. Because every day he'd drag his wife by the hair to the community hall and beat her up as if she were an animal, with his belt. Everyone came to watch. But nobody could go near and separate them. Every day, for some reason or another, there would be a quarrel between them. It always came to blows.

It seems when these two were getting married, just before the tali-tying, the priest asked Uudan, 'Are you willing to take this woman for your wife?' And Uudan, present there as the bridegroom, mind you, answered loudly, 'No, I'm not willing, saami.' At once the girl's father and uncles threatened and intimidated Uudan and forced him to agree; the tali-tying took place only after that. People used to say that it was because he was forced into marrying a woman he didn't like that he beat her like that every day.

Anyway, this Uudan knew how to play the flute really well. He would play on a bamboo pullaanguzhal really beautifully. Whenever there was a mike set, and singing and dancing in the hall, then Uudan would play his flute. It sounded lovely.

Yet he couldn't even write an 'a' or 'aa'. People said they could not understand how he had learnt to play the flute. Then, when an adult education scheme was started here, he went along with his slate in hand, and started learning to read and write. But his wife came rushing up in a great frenzy, shouting at him and abusing him saying, 'Chi, shameless fellow. Now, when you are at your last gasp you want to start studying, do you? You are going to become some kind of Collector or what?' Now he's been dead for some seven or eight years.

There's another man like that, known as Pig-Pavulu. His real name is Pavulu. I don't know why they call him Pig-Pavulu. Both he and his son can sing and dance brilliantly. Once or twice they had brought a troupe of women from Marudai, and put on a dance performance with records. They had also put on plays.

Pig-Pavulu's son was a great prankster. One time, at Easter, when the icons were held at shoulder level, and taken round in sapparam procession, the drummers were completely drunk and were stumbling about, scarcely able to play. At that point, this boy and four or five other youths joined together, plucked away the drum, the flute, and the conch from the musicians, took over the music, and walked in procession in front of the chariot. And, he played even better than the professional drummer.

Then there was Thavasi-Pethiya's son Pavulu. He was another who sang really well. Now he too had a group whom he accompanied on the vil. Sometimes he would hold story-and-song villuppaattu sessions by the bazaar. In fact, several people were excellent at dance and song and rhythm, though they didn't even have a whiff of learning.

Some people beat out an accompanying rhythm to the songs by holding a wide-mouthed clay pot against their bellies, and tapping on it with a small stone. It was really good to hear. You could do this with a clay pot and you could do it with a brass pot too. It sounded even more splendid when four or five people played in unison, or against each other. They always swayed their heads according to the beat. You'd want to keep watching them forever.

Even the little ones were good at singing and dancing. Even the bare-bottomed toddlers would sing out 'sanjanakka-sanjanakka' as they strummed away on broken clay pots strung with cattle-membrane, and they danced beautifully, never once losing the beat.

Women too sang. As they planted out paddy seedlings, or weeded the fields, or harvested the grain, they worked to the rhythm of their songs. They sang to their babies as they rocked them in their cradles. They sang to the young girls when they came of age. They sang dirges to their dead. After the Easter Pusai was said in the church, the women stood in a circle and sang: *Thervil varaare, theruvil varaare—Yesu thervil varaare, He is coming through our street, he is coming through our street—Yesu is coming in his chariot.*

They would sing this and dance a kummi, clapping hands. It was only after they did this that the sapparam procession was taken around our parts.

They sang teasing songs to the prospective bride and groom who were usually cross-cousins:

As I was grinding the masala, machaan
you peeped over the wall
What magic powder did you cast upon me?
I cannot lift the grinding stone any more.

At night, the young men went off to hunt in the mountain jungle with their hunting dogs. This was not just a pastime for them, though. Wild animals such as wild pigs and foxes often destroyed the crops in the fields. So they went to trap them. But they also set their dogs on wild rabbits and pigs and caught whatever they could find.

Once they caught a porcupine and tied it to the lamp-post in front of the community hall. That was the first time that I ever saw a porcupine. If they caught a wild pig, they would thrust it into the fire, burn off all its bristles, smear it with turmeric and wash it, decorate it with flowers, garland it, tie it high up in a bullock cart, and take it from street to street. Adults and children, we'd all follow the cart. The man who caught and killed the pig would receive a new veshti and shoulder cloth. Once it was taken through all the streets, it would be butchered, and the meat distributed to all the families. The entire village would be in high spirits that day. On one occasion they even managed to catch a deer. It was actually forbidden to kill deer or mountain goat. But if the forester was given a portion of the meat, he would turn a blind eye.

* * * *

Then there were celebrations for Christmas, New Year, Easter, and for the Chinnamalai festival. Nowadays, though, these celebrations are different. People seem to be more enthusiastic about going to the cinema than they are in Church affairs. After many years, I was at home this past New Year. From New Year's Eve onwards, the whole village was lively and bustling. All along the street, women who had soaked rice and lentil for dosai, idli, and paniyaaram were at their grindstones, talking and gossiping as they prepared the batter. They were calling out to each other in great excitement.

'Ei, Akka, Balendra's wife, are they going to butcher a cow tomorrow?' This was Ekalam.

'What a question, di! Is it likely that they won't slaughter a cow for the New Year?'

'In that case, sister-in-law, I'd better go and tell that macchaan to keep aside a couple of kilos of meat for us. Otherwise we won't get anything.' Saying this, Anthoni-Amma rushed off home in haste.

Michael-Amma was sitting on her stone pestle. Now she said, 'So many people of other castes eat beef secretly these days, it's getting more and more difficult for us to get any meat. All of them eat their fill, but see, it's only we people who are called low-caste.'

It must have been about nine at night. Over the mike at the community hall, there came a loud announcement that there would be a cinema show the following night, in celebration of the New Year. From the tiniest one, everyone was in a state of high excitement. They all waited impatiently for the hours to pass.

The next morning the whole street was astir. Absolutely bustling with joy. Someone was calling out her wares in a sing-song voice, and making good business: apples, oranges, grapes. What's this, I wondered as I went out to see, how is it that such expensive fruit is being sold along our street?

'Here, you with the oranges, come here, Amma.' I was surprised to hear so many voices summoning the fruit-seller eagerly.

Muthamma's son said, 'Amma, make sure you buy the fruit for the priest and for the Mother Superior at the same time.'

Then the daughter added, 'Look Amma, the members of Our Lady's Sabai have to make their gifts too; get enough for them as well.'

I understood what was going on only after that. At the start of the New Year, it was the custom for the entire congregation to go, family by family, both to the Mother Superior and to the priest, carrying gifts of fruit or biscuits. They would garland the priest and the Mother Superior and pay their respects. I realized that this was still happening. Even though our people had never tasted the fruit themselves, they somehow went through every effort to buy the fruit for the Church elders; they made their offering, knelt before them in all humility, and received the sign of the cross on their foreheads.

From our house too, we went to church carrying our gifts. On that day, because it was the New Year, there was a long queue in front of the confession box. The Pusai began at eight in the morning, and concluded, one way or another, at half-past ten.

During the Pusai, there was only one man who sang out loudly, while quite a few others accompanied him by beating out the rhythm on all sorts of objects. Suddenly there was a voice from the women's side, 'There isn't a soul even to sing the hymns. But there are ten fellows ready and willing to beat out the rhythm. Shameless fellows!' When she said this loud and clear, there was a quick burst of laughter in the church. But some people went, 'sh. . .sh' like a pack of snakes, and told them to be quiet.

At the very centre of the church, just where the priest had sprinkled holy water and left, a small urchin was standing, completely naked. He then began walking along the grille, pissing as he went. Goodness knows whether he thought he was sprinkling holy water around, just as the priest had done. He was holding on to himself exactly as if he was dribbling out kolam-flour.

A nun who saw him rose to her feet, went up to him and gave him four sharp blows to his back. The boy couldn't stand the pain and screamed out, whereupon his mother yelled, 'It's New Year's Day, and he's only a baby; should you hit him as if he has committed some kind of heinous sin?' And with this, she picked up the child and walked out of the church.

When the Pusai was over, there was a huge crowd at the priest's house. Not only did each family come with their offering, but many groups such as the Our Lady's Sabai, the Holy Childhood Sabai, the Good Death Sabai, and the Soldiers of God brought their gifts, too. We too went along with the crowd, pushed our way ahead, made our offerings, and came away. Whether we asked for it or not, the priest made the sign of the cross on every forehead, one after the other; upon those who knelt in front of him and those who fell down in full prostration.

One woman lamented, 'The priest who was here before this always gave us a couple of orange sweets, five or six holy pictures, and a new calendar when we came with our offering. This one just puts a cross on us and tells us to go away.' Everyone agreed with her, and they came away complaining about his miserliness.

'Ei, Akka, I asked the priest for a calendar, smiling sweetly at him all the time. He actually asked me for money, Akka. He says he'll only sell them. Just see how the times have changed.' Anthoni-Amma laughed as she said this.

At once the leader of the Our Lady's Sabai scolded everyone. 'Very well, don't stand about showing your teeth. Let's go to the convent now. Our sabai has to give Mother Superior her offering.' But it seems that the Reverend Mother also sent them away with the sign of the cross. Someone had asked her, 'Reverend Mother, please give us at least a holy picture.' And the Mother Superior had said, 'Have you given me some money in order to buy you holy pictures? Very well, now, you may all go home quickly without leaning on the walls or touching anything.'

Later, she summoned the leader of the sabai and carefully counted out just enough small drawstring cloth bags so that only those who had gone to see her that morning would receive one each. Later on there was a rumpus over this very thing.

'Children of whores, couldn't you have brought a bag for me too? Haven't I paid my seven rupees for the presentation, just like everyone else? All those others who never paid their fair share have gone and got drawstring bags, the wretches!' Tirusiluvam-Akka was shouting loud enough to make the whole street resound. Anyway, after that everyone took their share of meat, cooked and ate it, and then waited eagerly for the evening's cinema show.

* * * *

By seven in the evening, there was a huge crowd at the community hall. Schoolboys went along the street ringing a bell and announcing that the priest would be giving a special Blessing at the church because of the New Year. But not a soul went, for who would miss the picture and go to the Blessing instead?

The gossip was that the village Naataamai had hired the video recorder and deck and that there would be three shows going on throughout the night. Anthoni-Amma from next door came and told us, 'Periamma, they say there will be three shows on at different places. There will be a Rajnikant film at the shrine of St Sebastian, a Kamal Hasan film at the shrine of St Anthony, and an MGR film at the shrine of St Ignatius. Somehow or the other I have to see all three. Oh, why didn't they put on a Sivaji Ganesan film as well?' And she ran off to the community hall like the wind.

But even after ten at night, neither the equipment nor the films had arrived. The people who had been waiting for so long were desperately disappointed. It looked as if it was going to drizzle, besides. Nevertheless, everyone sat there in front of the dais, as if they had been nailed to the ground, praying to St Sebastian intermittently, to hold off the rain.

Then Chinnappan said, 'Well, what if we can't get the video equipment? Why can't we bring out Chittappa teacher's TV and show the picture in that?'

'How can we show a picture on someone's home TV, da? In that TV you can only see whatever is being transmitted from the stations.' It was Thomas who said this. Then Kalkundaan who was sitting in the crowd explained as best as he could. 'Say this TV is like your hand-radio. If you put in a tape and watch a video film, it's like using your radio like a tape recorder. But if you turn the knobs on a radio you can only listen to whatever is being broadcast through it. It's just like that. You turn the knob on the TV and then you can watch only what is being transmitted. But with a video deck, you can push in whatever picture you like, and watch that.'

Although it was past eleven, the cinema show had not arrived, so the crowds began to dissolve and people went away home. Then all of a sudden there was an announcement over the mike, that although the proper equipment had not arrived, they would show the film on a makeshift screen. Again people ran as fast as they could to find a decent spot in the community hall. In front of the dais, two poles had been planted upon which a white screen was fixed.

'Ei, Sevathi-Akka, they are setting up a screen show, it's going to be an MGR picture; come soon,' Amalorpavam called out, running as she went.

'Ei, cousin Vaikundam, what's the picture? Who's acting?'

'It's *Kudiyirunda Koil*, the temple they lived in. MGR and that Amma, Jayalalita, acted in it.' Everyone was delighted when that young man gave out this information.

At last the cinema show began at about twelve. Everyone shut up and there was silence. Before they showed the main film there was a small sequence showing MGR's bier being carried along the streets after he died. The audience joined in with sympathetic noises. After the long wait, everyone watched this scene, wholly absorbed by the tragedy. And at last, after all this, the film *Kudiyirunda Koil* began.

The next morning, I asked a few people what yesterday's film had been like.

'Oh, didn't you come? Oh what a fine picture it was. MGR played two roles. You should have seen how well Jayalalita acted. I can't tell you how beautiful she is. You know that bit where MGR and that Amma sing together? You know when they sing, *I tell you again not to go there; you must not go*, and the father comes and drives them away? I had to go to the toilet just then, I couldn't hold out any longer. I had to go and miss just that bit.'

Then she said that a certain Nambiyar, or someone with a similar name, made his appearance after that. He apparently turns up in many films, always playing a similar role, as the villain. In this film he has a daughter who strips off and dances about in that state. 'She doesn't seem to have any shame, Akka. But how can whores like that feel any shame?'

And so people set off on their different tasks, commenting on the film they had seen.

At Christmas, Easter, and on New Year's Day, people hang up posters of Rajnikant and Kamal Hasan here and there. Nobody seems to know what the festival is really about, or what it is celebrating. Different fan clubs will hang up these pictures during their competitions. They will set up loudspeakers in four or five different places and broadcast songs which seemed to wail and scream through the air. These are the pastimes of today.

Now, besides, there is a cinema of our own in our parts. People go and watch films there, every now and then. In the old days, the more educated of the young people would put on plays. Now you don't see any of that. They all go about having learnt a few things in a half-hearted way. In their spare time, the old folk play games such as aadupuli, a chess-like board game with three pieces as 'tigers' and twelve pieces as 'sheep', or they play cards. Many drink toddy or arrack and get into quarrels and fights.

Six

Whenever my father was due to come home on leave from the army, I'd be happy in one way, but also fearful in another way. Whenever he came home on leave, he brought lots of things to eat: grapes, apples, tins of biscuits, sweets, new clothes, tinned milk, tinned fish, and all sorts of exotic things. We'd look forward to eating all this. There was always plenty of good food to eat throughout the two months that he was at home. But for all the rest of the time, there would be nothing but kuuzh.

Usually we had rice and kuzhambu only in the evenings. Otherwise, it was some kind of kuuzh in the mornings and at midday. It would be a kuuzh appropriate to the season. To go with the kuuzh there would be something or the other—onions, groundnuts, moulded jaggery, green chillies. If there was a little money in hand, there might be a side dish of roasted and ground gram, or a pickle from the Nadar shop, or anything else we could buy. This pickle was usually hung up in packets in the shops. The shop owners would usually prepare this 'kadichukira' in their own homes and bring it to their shops. They used to make it full of flavour, with all sorts of good things like brinjals and red chillies. They'd give you five or ten paisa's worth, wrapped up in a banyan leaf. To this day, this relish is known as kadichukira. It always went very well with our kuuzh.

On Sundays we usually had a good meal. They butchered a cow exactly at the time when we returned from the morning Pusai. With our midday kuuzh we would be given a little of the meat in its plain stock. For this, the meat was just boiled with a touch of salt; but no masala whatever. Then in the evening there would be rice with a meat curry. On the day when they were cooking meat, we came home as soon as the prayers were over at church, without getting led away into anything else.

When the lake was full, the fish that was cheapest was the silebi kenda and the kenda. If they bought this fish and made a curry with it, we never could bear to go to the church in the evening. We could only make ourselves go after we had eaten the fish curry and rice. But there were times when there was nothing at all at home. My mother would somehow manage to relieve our hunger with a little leftover rice or kuuzh.

Every day when we left for school, we'd ask for two or three paise. This was our daily routine. We never forgot to ask for our spending money, just as soon as we were ready.

When my father was in the army, all those wars happened: the Pakistan war, the China war, the Bangladesh war. During those times, he was never able to send home any money. Nor did we ever get any letters. It was my mother who managed to look after us, by picking up some coolie work. We'd go to the lakeside in the evenings, pluck some wild greens like kuppaikira or thoyilukkira, and eat it with a quickly stirred and thickened ragi dough. Sometimes we boiled and ate drumstick leaves. During the school holidays, I'd find some work gleaning groundnuts, collecting firewood, picking up dry dung. Sometimes, we children would finish off whatever gruel or porridge there was. Then it was my mother who had to go hungry. Somehow we managed like this until I got to the eighth class.

It was after this that I was admitted into the hostel of a convent in the next village. It was a hostel which demanded quite a high fee. And I felt uncomfortable to stay there, although they fed us well. It was a really big school, too. A lot of children studied there. As for me, at first I didn't at all want to stay and study there. On the other hand, I was too scared to run away home. Before she left, my mother had threatened me that my elder brother would kill me if I ran away from school and returned home. Because there was no other way out, I gritted my teeth and stayed. And gradually, as time went on, everything worked out all right for me. A child from the Thevar street of our village joined the school at the same time as me. Within two days she ran off home.

Both in the hostel and in the school, the children wore all sorts of fine clothes, and they kept nice things to eat in their rooms. So I thought they must all be upper-caste children. My mother too had given me some fried groundnuts and puffed rice. I had put this aside for myself. I wondered to myself how it was that children belonging to other communities always had fine clothes and good food. I realized it was they who had the money. As for me, my community was low-caste; I had no money either. All the same, I thought, I would study hard and make good. So I worked really hard.

In my village, taking as evidence my skill at picking out the lice from her hair, my grandmother used to claim that I was going to be a really smart child. And whenever my elder brother wrote to me, he would say, 'You have lots of brains; it's as if a palmyra fruit has been thrust into a sparrow's head. Study well and gain lots of marks.' And so, gradually, I cared less and less about clothes. I went about my own business, telling myself this was the destiny that was given to me.

My father, who was still in the army, sent me money every month. He sent me more than I needed for my school and hostel fees. I had enough to buy and eat what I wanted; I was happy enough. On visitors' Sunday my mother would come, bringing cooked beef, or a curry she had made out of a chicken that she had bought and killed. She would also buy me lots of snacks. When she came, she would look through my hair for lice, then plait it for me and put flowers in it before she left. This made me very happy. I was at that school until the eleventh class, after which I returned home. Everyone had said I would gain good marks in the eleventh year public examinations, and I was pleased about this.

But then, my parents wanted me to stay back home saying there was no need for me to go to college or to study any further. In any case there was no money. Then, they said it would be difficult for me to find a husband in my community if I went in for further education. So they wrote off to a few places to find out about teacher training.

During those holidays, I went to see a nun who had taught me in the eleventh class. She really grieved to think of me sitting at home without studying. She spoke to my mother and made a fuss, complaining that she must not stop a girl who really enjoyed her studies from going further with it. When my mother said that she didn't have the money, this nun made her pawn the earrings she was wearing, then took me by the hand, and sent me to a college with the money. And I, firm in the resolve that I would carry on with my studies one way or another, arrived at the college with just the clothes I was wearing, and admitted myself into the hostel.

For a whole week I went around in the same skirt, jacket, and daavani. All my classmates looked at me as if I was some outlandish creature. Some of them asked me, Did I only possess one set of clothing? Didn't I have any others? I felt deeply humiliated. I told them my mother was bringing my belongings, and I went to the hostel and wept. Meanwhile, my father wrote to me from the army, very abusively, 'You listened to the nuns' advice and joined college; so now ask them to give you the money; go on, go to them.' I didn't wish to go back home, though. There was this certain something in me that urged me to go on and complete my studies. That's why I endured all the shame and humiliation and stayed on.

When they saw my marks, when they realized how alert I was at my work, the teachers and nuns praised me. And a week later, my mother brought me my clothes, my box, and my bedding. After this, my classmates began to be friendlier towards me. They were surprised that I got the first mark in all the tests. The teachers also said, 'Look at this one who joined late, how well she is doing!' After this, I didn't bother about clothes and jewellery, and went about my work in my own way.

Some of the students asked me, 'Why aren't you wearing anything in your ears and about your neck? You don't even have chappals on your feet', they said. It was true that almost all of them came to college wearing all kinds of trinkets, and with fine clothes. But where would I go for such things? I even pawned my small earrings in order to pay my examination fees. And my clothes certainly weren't anything much.

At home, we bought new clothes twice a year. Once, for Christmas. Then, for the Chinnamalai festival which was celebrated at the hill grotto of Our Lady. Apart from those two occasions, we never bought anything. We had to manage with these two sets of clothes. I began to collect my elder sister's cast-offs. And so I got by for four years.

In my fourth year, the time neared for College Day. College Day was always celebrated on a grand scale. All the final year students were invited to a party, which they attended dressed in silk saris and decked out in their best things. As for me, I didn't have a single decent sari to my name. I didn't know what to do. I didn't want to borrow a sari from someone or the other and wear that. And on that particular day, I couldn't take myself away elsewhere, nor would they have allowed me. So at last, I made up my mind and went and locked myself up in the bathroom. I wanted to weep and weep when I considered my plight. And I realized how deeply shamed one can be for the lack of a few rupees in one's hand.

A friend of mine from a Naicker family had said to me, 'You could have written home and asked them to send you a silk sari.' So, were there silk saris growing in a garden in my home? She couldn't have known the truth—that there was no one in my home who possessed a silk sari. I could not have asked them to buy me a silk sari either. There was no money to throw away on a sari. So I hid in the bathroom until the party was over.

It was like that at the institution where I studied for my B.Ed. as well. I consoled myself that there were any number of people who were in a worse plight than myself.

Once I finished my B.Ed. and started to work, life became comfortable enough. It was really good to earn enough money every month and to go about independently, and as I pleased. I could buy the sari or jacket that took my fancy, and wear it. I could go wherever I wanted to go. I could buy and eat what I liked. I could even have a few pieces of jewellery made for myself. I became aware that if you have a little money in your hands you can gain some authority, and status, and prestige. Is it for nothing that they say, 'Wealth flows even as far as Pataala Lokam?' And I realized that those who have the cash to spend can always afford to live in comfort.

But our people, however hard they toil, never seem to be able to have that cash in hand. They work so hard that they wear themselves out like potsherds. They live on gruel every day, they wear nothing more than a couple of rags, they own neither property nor land nor even a decent house to live in. In such conditions they work, and only for the good of the rich. How can they even hope for luxuries? Even I could, in the end, contrive to live a life of moderate comfort. I realized that if only the children on my street acquired a little education and found jobs, then they too could live reasonably well. But then, how are they to educate themselves? The struggle to fill their bellies is their main struggle, after all.

It was this train of thought that led me to the foolish desire that I could become a nun and enter a convent, and in that way work hard for other children who struggled as I had done. There was a desire in my heart to help other children to better themselves, as I, born into the same community, had been able to do, because of my education. I really wanted to teach such children. But I understood, after I entered the order, that the convent I entered didn't even care to glance at poor children, and only wished to serve the children of the wealthy. In that convent, they really do treat the people who suffer from poverty in one way, and those who have money in their pockets in a totally different way.

Before they become nuns, these women take a vow that they will live in poverty. But that is just a sham. The convent does not know the meaning of poverty. When the bell rang, there was a meal. And was it just rice that we were served? There was always food of all kinds. By turns, at each meal there was meat, fish, or eggs. There was always an abundance of fruit and a variety of vegetables. There was a comfortable room to live in. Each room had a bedstead, a fan, table and chair, and drinking water. The school was close by the convent. You could reach it in a few paces, and run home as you chose. No need to catch a bus, be pushed and shoved among crowds, and arrive home breathless from all the rush. At ten in the morning there was coffee and snacks. At twelve, a hot meal. Once again tea and snacks at four in the afternoon, and a hot meal at seven.

Yes, there was every comfort and convenience there. One could have stayed there comfortably, with enough to eat, clothes to wear, and the chance to travel to different places. But I began to think, soon after I entered the convent, Chi, is this all there is to the life of renunciation? Is there an understanding of poverty here?

The school was full of children from wealthy families. The nuns from the convent matched their attitude and behaviour to the power and prestige of those families. The more I watched this, the more frustrated I felt. My mind was disturbed. My conscience was battered and bruised. At last I asked myself, is this the life for me? I left the convent and went home, utterly weary and dispirited.

Although I went away home with a certain amount of bravado, it turned out to be difficult enough. I had lost the job that I had. I had no money at all. I didn't even have enough clothes to wear. My mind was full of anguish. But more than anything else, it was as if everything had changed when I came out. As if I had been blindfolded and then turned out into a forest, I struggled to find my way.

And though they took me back at home, I felt uncertain and confused. Convent life had changed me fundamentally. I who had once been bold had become an extremely timid person, fearful of everything, ready to burst into tears, and without any strength. I felt orphaned, as if I had no family. I felt too shy even to communicate with people in a normal way. Sometimes I even thought to myself that it would be better to be dead and gone rather than carry on living like this.

Today I am like a mongrel, wandering about without a permanent job, nor a regular means to find clothes, food, and a safe place to live. I share the same difficulties and struggles that all Dalit poor experience. I share to some extent the poverty of the Dalits who toil far more painfully through fierce heat and beating rain, yet live out their lives in their huts with nothing but gruel and water. Those who labour are the poorest of the poor Dalits. But those who reap the rewards are the wealthy, the upper castes. This continues to happen in my village to this day.

Life is difficult if you happen to be poor, even though you are born into the upper castes. When this is the case, the condition of those who are born into the Paraya community, as the poorest of the poor, struggling for daily survival, doesn't need spelling out. Such people have just enough time, if they wake up well before cock-crow, to sweep their front yard, collect water, swallow some gruel if possible, and rush off to work as best as they can. In the midst of all this, how can they be expected to look after their children and make sure they go to school?

In the face of such poverty, the girl children cannot see the sense in schooling, and stay at home, collecting firewood, looking after the house, caring for the babies, and doing household chores. As soon as the boys have picked up a smattering of learning, they wander off to look after the goats and the cattle. If you look at our streets, they are full of small children, their noses streaming, without even a scrap of clothing, rolling about and playing in the mud and mire, indistinguishable from puppies and piglets.

But the wealthy live off the labour of the poor, like leeches, and their children eat well and fatten; they wear fine clothes, attend good schools, take up high positions, and earn more and more money. It seems that our society is divided into those who toil and those who sit down and feast. They have separated out those whom they consider unfit to touch, pushed them to one side and marginalized them; they make them work like machines yet abuse them unjustly, never allowing them to make any progress. I don't know when such atrocities will ever end. Is it likely that he who finds his comfort by exploiting us will ever change, or ever allow the system to change?

And there are many who patiently accept and endure their hard lives, consoling themselves that this was the destiny given them, that they cannot see a way to change the caste they were born into, nor the poverty that is part of that caste, nor indeed the humiliation of it all. On the other hand there are a few others who know that this is neither our fate nor our destiny, and who are making efforts to challenge these atrocities. But you see, our mental firmness doesn't match the influence and authority that money-power wields. For how many days can one fight in the name of justice and strength when one is hungry and thirsty? Even for a daily meal we have to depend on someone else. We dance to someone else's tune, even for a serving of rice. And, of course, knowing this fully well the wealthy control and crush Dalits.

You see this attitude not only among the common people in the society about us. Far worse is the attitude within our own Church. They have made use of Dalits who are immersed in ignorance as their capital, set up a big business, and only profited their own castes. In the churches, Dalits are the most in numbers alone. In everything else, they are the least. It is only the upper-caste Christians who enjoy the benefits and comforts of the Church. Even amongst the priests and nuns, it is the upper castes who hold all the high positions, show off their authority, and throw their weight about. And if Dalits become priests or nuns, they are pushed aside and marginalized first of all, before the rest go about their business. It is because of this that even though Dalits like me might wish to take up the path of renunciation, we find there is no place for us there.

Seven

When I look back upon all these years that have gone by, I realize that the bhakti and belief I had in God has changed in a curious way. I am myself surprised by this.

When I lived at home as a child, the people who taught me about devotion to God were my mother, Paatti, my teachers and the nuns, and later on, the priests. I believed entirely in what they told me. I prayed exactly as I was taught.

There were catechism classes every evening at church. After school was done, within a short while, we would cover our heads with a piece of cloth and set off to the church. Sometimes we'd be ravenously hungry. We'd long for something to munch as we walked along our way. Sometimes we would soak a little broken rice and carry that in our clothes or shirt pockets, and munch on that. On our way we'd see all sorts of things being sold at the bazaar by the oil-press. But we never had any money. So we'd stand and watch a while and then move on.

In the morning, dew or rain, we had to rise at dawn and go to morning Pusai. We'd clean our teeth in a haphazard way, fling a piece of cloth over our heads, and run. It was at cock-crow, somehow, that you were most deeply asleep. Yet it was at that hour we had to wake up and run. It used to be a torment just to get up. We'd scarcely wash our faces and make haste. When the lake was swollen with water, it was near impossible to go. It was usually very cold then. However much you were shaken awake, all you wanted to do was to turn over and go to sleep, you just couldn't bear to get up. But really there was nothing else for it; however hard you resisted, you just had to go. If you didn't go, the next day at assembly you were beaten by the priest or by a teacher. Nor were these ordinary blows. The cane fell on us with the sharpness of a whip. It left great weals. Enough to be reminded of those blows. Then we'd spring out of our beds at last.

From the time I was a child, I found it easy to learn by rote. I also found I had a good memory. So I was always in good form in the catechism class. Whenever there was a test on the Scriptures, I always won the first prize.

When I was studying in the second class, a priest who was a white man came to visit our school. He was of a good height, and had a long, brilliantly white beard. All of us were curious just to touch him. The Sister asked each of us to repeat various prayers. She asked us to repeat the Six Perfections of God, the Lord's Prayer, the Hail Mary, and the Creed. I was the only one there who could say all of them correctly. The priest lifted me up and kissed me and gave me a five paisa piece. I was pleased first of all that the priest touched me and lifted me up. That he should have kissed me and even given me the money made my heart leap with joy. I took the coin and tucked it away carefully in my skirt. I wanted to show them at home. That's why.

I made my First Communion while I was still in the second class. When I was in the third, the Bishop of Madurai came to our village. I was confirmed then.

When I went to study at the primary school run by nuns, the Sisters entrusted me to lock up and to open the parish church. I would do all such jobs as going to the church and bringing the vases over at school time, polishing them, and then putting them back after the Sisters had arranged them with flowers. I always took one of the other children with me because I was frightened to go inside the church by myself. I felt a bit braver if there was someone with me.

If ever I had to stay alone in the church, my insides would quake. Because just at those times I would remember the stories that the Sisters had told us in Scripture lessons about the Devil.

They had told us that if we kept on committing sins, the Devil would put them all down in a long list written into a big notebook, which he would show to God. Sister said, in the Scripture lesson, that if we committed so many sins that the notebook actually filled up, then he would peel the skin off our backs and write our sins there. I would recall this always at the precise moment when I was alone in the church. I imagined the Devil busily writing down my sins, and when the notebook was completely full, coming towards me to rip the skin off my back. I would see very clearly and within my vision, the dark Devil that I had been shown in pictures, with a long tail, and with sharp horns, nails and teeth, coming towards me to show me the notebook in which my sins were written down. I would die of fear then. But usually I forgot about it when I left the church and came outside.

The nuns never seemed to tell us any cheerful stories. It was always stories of the Devil. They told us about the Devil wandering about with a pair of balances, with the sins we had committed in one pan weighed against the merit we had earned in the other. Every time I went near the church, I would be stupefied with terror, imagining the Devil with his balance, yelling above my head. I could actually see my load of sins pulling the pan downwards.

In order bring down my pan of good deeds I did everything that the Sisters told me to do. I obeyed them in all things. I repeated my prayers very often. But in spite of all this, my pan of sins continued to be the heavier one. They said you could actually see the Devil with your own eyes. That is what really scared me. We used to imagine the Devil to be exactly like the creature in the advertisement of Onida TV. Only the real Devil would be even more terrifying to look at, we thought, black as the night. I'd be shaken to the core at the very thought.

The Sisters told us that if we sinned greatly, it delighted the Devil and made our guardian angel very sad. So if ever I told a small lie, if I stole a stick or pencil, if at home I didn't obey my parents or elders, if I wasn't good at school, I'd see in front of my eyes the Devil wandering about with his balances, laughing happily, and my guardian angel wretched and weeping. I too would want to weep then. However much I wanted to forget this scene or to wipe it out, I could not. It just appeared before my eyes all the more intensely.

Before I made my First Communion, they taught me most carefully about making my confession. For many days I simply repeated what they taught me to confess. Every week I went to the confession box, knelt down and reeled off the formula I had learnt by heart.

'I praise the Lord Omnipotent. Bless me Saami, for I have sinned. It is a week since I made my last confession. I lied four times; I stole five times; I have not obeyed my elders; I was daydreaming in church. I repent these and those sins that I have forgotten, saami.' This was always the formula.

The priest would tell me to say three Hail Marys as my punishment, and give me a blessing out loud. We had to get up from our knees, go into the church, and complete our penances immediately. It was always scary to leave the priest's bungalow and enter the darkness of the church. Every time I finished my confession, I would set off for the church, trembling, and at a half-run. We'd repeat the prayers that the priest had asked us to say, end with an Act of Contrition, and then run home.

When we received the host at Communion, we were not supposed to touch it either with our teeth or our fingers. The Sisters had warned us that even if it stuck to our palates, we should only move it gently with our tongues and swallow it. The Sisters had told us over and over again that Jesus was inside that host, we should not bite Him, nor should we touch the host with our sinful hands. For some time I did as they told me. It was very embarrassing when it got stuck to my palate. Often it was difficult to shift it gently with my tongue. It also took an age to do this. I always worried about how I would manage to say the appropriate prayers after Holy Communion. So I always tried very hard to swallow it down somehow.

It was very funny, actually. I would have to hide my mouth behind my head-cloth and then scrape my tongue against my palate pushing my head to one side with the effort, and somehow manage to shift it in that way. At the same time I had to keep watching from the corner of my eye in case anyone observed my antics; particularly, of course, the Sisters.

For a long time I had a perverse wish to try touching the host with my finger. So one day, hiding myself well behind my head-cloth, I managed it at last. And it didn't happen at all as the nuns had threatened. They had said that if I touched it, blood would flow down my hand. I removed my finger and examined it. Nothing. I told myself that the Sisters had spoken empty words. But I couldn't say that to anyone else. I wanted to. But I was afraid that if I did so, it would be common knowledge that I had touched the host wilfully. So I didn't say anything then.

It seems that in some village or the other, one lad had bitten into the host. From that very moment that morning, blood streamed from his mouth. It didn't stop throughout the day...the Sisters told us this story too. I wanted to test that out too, so another time I put my head-cloth against my mouth, and terrified by what I was doing, bit, chewed, and swallowed. I wiped my mouth with my cloth and looked at it. No blood at all. Then I knew that this too had been an empty threat by the Sisters. I couldn't tell anyone about this either. So it was in this way that I grew up in devotion and belief.

When I was in the third class, I was confirmed. They had told me that during the confirmation service, the Bishop would slap my cheek. They said that it was at that moment that the Spiritus Sanctus would descend upon me. As the Bishop neared me, I kept opening and shutting my eyes in expectation of the slap, so when he caught me a resounding blow upon my cheek, I wasn't aware of any Spiritus Sanctus descending. Still, I kept my head bowed in devotion. I still want to laugh when I remember this.

When I started going to the convent school, I belonged to the Baalar Sabai, the Holy Childhood Movement. On Sundays, we pinned on our Baalar Sabai badges before attending Pusai. We were hugely proud of these badges. Then after Pusai, there was a special service for the Baalar Sabai. There used to be a Baalar Sabai day once a year. Then you had to contribute money every now and then for something or the other. That's the thing I remember most.

There was usually a catechism class on Sunday evenings. When that was over, there was the Blessing in the church. This Blessing would seemingly go on for hours and hours. The priest would come, give his sermon, and ask any number of questions as time went on and on. We small children would be so sleepy, we could scarcely keep our eyes open. If your eyes drooped even in the slightest, the Sister sitting nearby would land a stinging blow on your back. Though we tried to keep our eyes open in fear of that blow, in a short while it would be impossible. One by one we'd drop to to the floor.

As we grew a little older, the Sisters stopped beating us. But they'd give us a sharp pinch. That hurt even more. They seemed to grow their nails for the sole purpose of pinching us. The trouble was that just a little after we had been given a sharp nip, our heads would start nodding again. Sometimes when the priest saw this happening, he would ask the Sisters to slap us. Who should we have feared the most? It seemed impossible to control our urge to sleep. Once when I was dozing off like this and the Sister slapped me, I was so startled that I wet myself. She gave me a few extra blows for that. I screamed out so loudly that my mother came, cleaned me up, and carried me away.

Because I was good at reciting the litany, the Sisters made me teach the appropriate prayers to the girls who were preparing to get married. A catechist gave lessons to the prospective grooms at the church. After I had taught them for two or three weeks, the Sister would come and test the girls. If they could not say the prayers properly, it was I who got the scolding.

One day, when I was repeating the prayers, Sister turned up suddenly. I was so startled by this, and became so nervous that I made a mistake and changed a line that I was saying out loud. Almost the first thing that she did when she came right inside was to give me a knock on my forehead. I happen to have a big, wide forehead. And I nearly died of the pain. My forehead began to swell up where she struck it. But she wouldn't let me off even after that. I continued to repeat the prayers, weeping as I did so. On that day, I thought to myself secretly, that when I grew up I would pick up a stone and fling it at this Sister. I also thought to myself that I would never attend a catechism class or go to a Church service ever again. My anger abated a little with this thought. But before I grew up, that Sister left our village and was transferred elsewhere.

In this way, we went to Pusai every day in the morning, and to catechism and prayers in the evening. And in school, there were Scripture lessons for the Christian children and Moral Education for the Hindu children. I always gained good marks at Scripture. I even won prizes.

When we went to school or to church we had to walk some distance, past several streets. The church, the school, the convent and the priests' bungalow were all in places where the upper-caste communities lived. Most of the children attending the school were from our streets. All the same, all these children had to walk the distance there in order to study. There were only few upper-caste Christian children. For them, the church, the school, the convent, and the priests' house were all close at hand. There was no necessity for them to walk any distance. It was we who had to do that, through pouring rain and beating sun. What's more, often it was just the lights in our street that wouldn't work. Nobody would take any notice of this fact. In the darkness and the mire, you had to watch out for shit as you came and went. Perhaps the priests and the Sisters chose to live elsewhere because of the filthy conditions here; I don't know.

When I was studying in the school which the priests ran, from the sixth to the eighth class, they pulled down the old church and began work on a new one. So they began to dig the ground behind the old church in order to lay the new foundations. Some of us used to go there from our handwork class in order to shovel out the earth from the pits. One day when I was there, I could make out a skeleton against the walls of the pit. Two or three others saw it along with me, and we were all stunned with terror. Then another girl came along and told us a fascinating string of stories: that this was the skeleton of a former priest who had been buried here; he had been canonized and was now a saint and in heaven.

And not just that, either. She added that because this was the skeleton of a priest, if we took it and kept it as a relic, it would enable us to study well. We'd be granted anything we prayed for, she said. And as she was telling us all this, she helped herself to two or three of the teeth. At once the rest of us helped ourselves to whatever we could take from the skeleton. Of course we left the bigger bones alone. Anyway we couldn't carry those away. But we picked up all the little bones and teeth and put them carefully into our geometry boxes. Every day we prayed to the teeth: I don't want to be beaten by Teacher; I want to study well; I want to be clever. We prayed for all sorts of things like that.

A few days went by. One evening all of us in my family were sitting together at home, studying and reading. The science teacher had asked us to make a couple of diagrams. As I was drawing them, my elder sister saw the teeth in my box and asked, 'How did you get all these teeth, di? From where did you pick them up?' Immediately, my elder brother, my younger sister, my mother, and Paatti, all began asking me one question after another. So I told them all about it.

They all laughed heartily. My mother and Paatti told me emphatically that those were no priest's teeth, that the priests were never buried there, but that sometime ago, a man who had worked in the priests' kitchen had died and was known to have been buried there. They said that in all likelihood those teeth were his and that I must throw them out. But I didn't have the heart to do it. I had placed such devotion on those teeth. I even had some fear that it might be a sin if I threw them out. And in the end I didn't do it. It was Annan, my older brother, who took the lot and flung them on the rubbish heap. The next day when

I went to school, I told the others all about it. And they too decided, fearfully, to fling their bones away. We took them and cast them away with a feeling of repulsion, exactly the opposite of the respect and devotion in which we had held them, and we ran home without once looking back. I have been caught up in blind belief such as this, and come away from it.

In those days, every evening there would be family prayers at home. As soon as we came home from church in the evening, there would be prayers at home. Hunger would tear at our insides. But my mother would say sternly that there would be food only after prayers. If there was something like fish or meat waiting, we could never concentrate on the prayer, anyway. And sometimes we would insist obstinately that we had to eat first. If we said our prayers after dinner, though, everyone would fall asleep. Hence the rule that dinner always came after prayers.

Even if the rest of us said our prayers only out of a sense of duty, my mother always covered her head properly and prayed in the most rapt and tender-hearted fashion. Whenever I think of my mother, it is this image of her, so often seen in my childhood, that appears before my eyes. After prayers, we sang hymns out of the hymn-book. But whatever we sang or did not my mother never forgot to sing, *My heart, come, let us worship; the Lord is everlasting bliss.* When the singing ended, we would eat.

When I was in the sixth class, our house was electrified. Until then, we only used kerosene-oil lamps. When we first got electricity, we used to love switching the lights on and off. There were even quarrels about it at home. Even Paatti would keep switching the lights on and off unnecessarily and then laughing like a child. She would keep repeating, in wonder, 'Just see what a magical thing this current is, which they've gone and discovered. As soon as I tap this thing, the current catches in a trice and lights the lamps.' She was overjoyed because the current never ran out the way that oil did.

In Paatti's house there was just the head of a Baby Jesus. It seems that the image of the Baby Jesus fell down in the church and broke, and so they had thrown the pieces out. But Paatti brought away just the head, very carefully, and kept it in her house. Whenever I went to her house, I would take the head and hold it in my lap, and kiss it. I'd take it to the street and show it to all the children there, so that they too could kiss it. Paatti would get really cross with me. She'd say that I would break it. Much later, when Paatti lay in bed ill, my younger brother took it, painted it in crazy colours and turned it into a doll's head. He didn't have an urge to show it the respect and devotion that I did.

In our house there were several pictures and icons of Jesus, Our Lady, St Joseph, St Anthony, St Sebastian, St Ignatius, Archangel Michael, the Holy Family, and the Crucifixion. There were several versions of Our Lady in any case; different pictures of Our Lady of Perpetual Succour, Our Lady of Poondi, Our Lady of Velankani, Our Lady of Sorrows. Once our house was electrified, we had a plug put in next to the pictures, so that a bulb would light up beside them. But at that time, I didn't know much about electric plugs. I only knew how to switch the lights on and off.

One day, as I was coming home from morning service, I stole a couple of hibiscus flowers from the garden of our teacher, whose house was just next to the church. If we were caught doing this they would never let us go. So we used to climb the compound wall very stealthily, and pick them. The flowers hung just over the wall. I wanted to bring the flowers and offer them to the picture of Jesus. But there was no convenient place to put them. Until my eyes fell on the plug.

As there were three good holes in the plug, I began by tucking one of the flowers by its stem into the first hole. Immediately I felt a tingle pulling all along my arm. I couldn't understand why it had happened. Anyway, I then tucked the second flower into the next hole. Again I felt the tug along my arm. When this happened the second time, I realized it was the electric current, pulling. At once I was frightened and I thought to myself, I'm done for now; God is allowing the current to tug at me like this because I stole the flowers and brought them here. Immediately I said a small prayer. Fearfully, I spoke out loud and said I would never again steal flowers and bring them there like this. Then I climbed down and went away. I had such a certainty of belief in those days.

* * * *

There is a mountain adjacent to our village. It seems that long ago, Our Lady made an appearance there. Once long ago, the parish priest of this place set off by bullock cart to the nearby village, to say Pusai there. In those days, they didn't have the buses that run now. So, as he was travelling by cart, it seems night fell. He was on a path through the forest at the time. Apparently the priest told the cart man to drive on anyway, because they had only a little further to go.

After a particular point, they say the bullocks refused to move. The cart man did his best to lead the animals forward. But they simply would not go any further. However hard he tried to urge them on, they refused even to take a single step forward. At last the priest gave up, thinking to himself what a wretched hour it was for the beasts to be acting in so stubborn a manner; so they stopped right there, and the priest went to sleep inside the cart.

It was a lonely place, with no sound nor trace of human beings. It was dense with trees. They heard the incessant buzz of bees. Both priest and cart man were terrified in their hearts. The priest fell asleep, repeating the rosary to himself.

They say it came to midnight. The priest lay asleep and dreaming. In his dream the Mother of God appeared to him and told him that he must build a church for her in that place. They say he woke up then and asked, 'Mother, where should I build it?' And he saw her standing at a little distance from where the cart had stopped, in all her grace and beauty. Around her there shone such a dazzling light. The next instant, amazingly, she had disappeared.

After that, it seems the priest could not sleep at all. He sat up until dawn broke, saying his rosary. At dawn, he woke up the cart man and asked him to go to the village where they were bound. And in the morning, the bullocks moved on in their customary way. He himself was surprised, they say. Then, it seems, the priest told the cart man all that had happened in the night. And they set about building a church there, straightaway. And my father too helped in the construction work as the church went up. This is how I've heard the older folk tell the story of the vision granted by Our Lady, and of how the church came to be built. That place is known as Chinnamalai, little mountain.

On the first Friday of every month, there used to be a Pusai at Chinnamalai. We school children would get together and set off walking there on Thursday evening, with our packed meals. There was a distance of about five or six miles between our village and the mountain. Before we left, we'd ask them at home to give us a little spending money. On the way we'd buy murukku, ice-candy, candyfloss, jelly sweets, guava, and cucumber, and we'd eat these things and chatter as we walked on.

In the evening, there would be a rosary at the church. At the end of that, we'd sit down and eat some of the food that we had brought. We'd keep the rest for the next morning. Then we'd spread our cloths on the church floor and sleep right there. If it was the season for ripe tamarind, we'd roast the ripe pods in the flame of the lighted candles and eat them. Otherwise, we'd spit on a stone and grind down raw tamarind, scrape the paste off and lick it. It would make our tongues blister. But we wouldn't leave off even then. It used to be great fun to climb the banyan trees there, and swing ourselves by holding on to the aerial roots. It was a good place. We'd also play with each other, clambering up and down the rocks. There were hills all about us. They were so beautiful. And the air always felt fresh, with a fine breeze blowing.

The next morning we'd wake up, clean our teeth with red-brick powder, wash our faces, and go to Pusai. Even while Pusai was being celebrated, some people would start arriving by the morning bus. We'd keep a look out during Pusai and check on the people who were arriving. As soon as Pusai was over, we'd go over to the icon of the crucified Christ which was in a mountain cave nearby, singing the hymn, *Yesuvin mathura thiru irudiyame, Sweet Sacred Heart of Jesus* all along the way, and say a prayer there. After we had put our offering in the collection box, we'd sit down to eat the rest of our packed rice. When we had finished, we'd pluck some leaves from the neem and tamarind trees to bring home in our tiffin carriers. All the older women used to do that. So we children used to do it too, in imitation of them. They said that these leaves were pure and holy leaves; they were good as medicine, too. If we kept them at home, we wouldn't get insect bites. If they were tucked above the entrance to the house, into the door-frame, no pey, pisaasu, nor ill-wind would come near.

After the Pusai was over, we would return home, walking all the way. By that time, the sun would be burning hot. We never wore chappals or anything of that sort. Even the dust would be scorching. We'd run a little, walk a little, sit under the shade for a while, and so at last we'd arrive home. The school usually gave us a holiday that day.

Apart from going up the Chinnamalai every month, we also celebrated the Chinnamalai festival every year in the month of May. Many people from the villages round about came to the festival. The flag was raised nine days before the festival, and the celebration took place on the ninth day in the evening and on the tenth day.

On the ninth day, from dawn, people would arrive in endless rows, by bullock cart, or on foot, or in buses. And they would bring with them a rooster, or a goat, or a pig which would be slaughtered at the mountain, besides firewood, pots and pans, and all the ingredients that they needed for cooking.

Chinnamalai, at that time, would be all animated, bustling with life. All around the church they would have set up canopies decorated with plantain trees, and lit up with tube lights. Heaven knows how the stall-keepers got wind of it, but they always turned up exactly two days ahead, cleared the ground and set up shop.

The stalls were always set up in a row: flower stalls, bangle stalls, stalls selling fruit, stalls with icons and images, and stalls selling idli-dosai and other snacks. There would also be a brisk petty-trade in sweet toddy, palm fruit, tender coconut, vadai, ices, halwa, kesari, and payasam.

The press of the crowds would be unbearable. All the carts and bullocks would be tied together, to one side. Cattle and chickens, unaware that they would be slaughtered soon, would be eating and squawking and crying aloud. Wherever you glanced, there would be people shouting out to each other and strolling about. Nowadays, though, it's not like that at all. In those days, the crowds were such there wasn't the space even to drop a til seed!

In the evening there would be a rosary and prayers in the church. Those who managed to squeeze inside the church would pray there. The rest would go to sleep. Young men would wander about the shops wearing new clothes, their hair slicked down with oil. Young women too would be in new clothes, with flowers in their hair, all gossip and giggles.

Older people would sit in the same place the whole day, pounding betel nut for chewing, keeping guard over the family's goods, and making sure that no one else was likely to take over their spot. From time to time, the babies lying in makeshift hammocks strung from pandal posts or branches of trees, would mewl and scream. For sometime nobody would hear them because of the noise all around. Only if they noticed the bouncing and tossing of the hammocks would the old women realize that the babies were crying. Then they would rock them to sleep again.

Very early in the morning there would be a sapparam procession of the holy images. Drummers, who had hardly slept at all, would walk ahead, beating on their drums, followed by a few men carrying petromax lamps. After that came the men carrying the icons. The procession went all around. Now and then they would let off crackers. Sometimes there would be firework displays as well. Only a few people followed on in the procession, though. Four or five priests still waited in the confession boxes. But how was one to confess anything in the midst of all that noise? The priest couldn't hear what we said, nor could we hear what he told us to do. All the same, because I thought it was my duty to do so, I too would stand along with all the others in the queue, and make my confession when it was my turn. If not, my mother and Paatti would scold me for not making my confession on such a holy day. So I always went along with them.

On the previous evening, people would have brought out their packed rice, and perhaps bought some vadai to eat before they dropped off to sleep. In the morning there would be a Pusai at the church. Even those who were half-asleep would somehow stumble in and take Communion at that hour. If they didn't take Communion then, it would only be possible to do so at the seven o'clock Pusai at the grotto. If they decided to go to the seven o'clock Pusai, then they would not be able to cook in the early morning. So somehow they would push and shove and manage to attend the early Pusai.

At seven o'clock, there was the Pusai at the grotto. We called it 'Guga Pusai'. The Pusai would proceed steadily, up above. Rising from the base of the hill, people would be seated in colourful row upon row; I always found this a beautiful sight. In the grotto, right at the top, two or three priests said Pusai in joint celebration. You had to be really smart to climb up and take Communion there. It was so steep and slippery all the way up. Still, we'd manage it somehow.

As soon as the Guga Pusai began, people here and there would put together their stone hearths, and start their cooking. Soon there would be smoke-clouds everywhere. It was piteous to hear the cries of the chicken and goat as they were slaughtered. Particularly it was the roosters that always seemed to make enough noise to awaken all the villages round about. Those who butchered calves or pigs would sell some of the meat to others. Those who hadn't brought their own firewood went around gathering twigs and thorny sticks. Some men would climb up trees and cut down withered old branches. By the time the rice was boiled, the kuzhambu cooked and taken off the fire, everyone would be ravenous. They used to spread out some straw, lay a damp cloth on top, spread the drained rice over that and let it cool. The smallest children, too hungry to wait, would scoop up the rice and eat it straight away.

Between ten and eleven, everyone would sit down in rows and feast until they were ready to drop. Then, before everyone had quite finished eating, beggars and nari-kuravan gypsies would crowd about us, scarcely allowing us to put food into our mouths. Once the feasting was over, one way or another, all the leftover rice, kuzhambu, and curry would be divided up and given away as charity to all those who begged. Then, in the heat of the afternoon, the bullock carts would be yoked and we would arrive home at sunset.

All this still happens year after year. Yet it seems that the devotion to Our Lady is manifested chiefly in choosing and wearing new clothes, and feasting on a newly slaughtered chicken or goat. And so it goes on. I hear that in these days they brew toddy and liquor in the hills surrounding the church. People arrive drunk and start brawls which can turn into outright and vulgar fights.

Until I entered the convent, I too went to Chinnamalai every festival day and joined in the worship. As a small child, the extent of my piety lay in the pleasure of receiving new clothes, riding in the cart, eating snacks, enjoying the feast, and buying icons, bangles, and toys. When I was a little older, it was still only the pleasure of wearing new clothes, and meeting my friends and sauntering about with them that drew me there. But when I developed some common sense and discrimination, it began to strike me that rather than jostle among the crowd in the name of the festival, I would much prefer to worship at home. After I joined the convent, I didn't get another opportunity to attend this particular festival. Nor did I think about it and regret it.

In my village, they celebrated Easter in a grand manner. There usually was a house-to-house collection for the festival, and a grand celebration with procession and drums. But it was just us, the Dalit Christians, who contributed to the festival. The Nadars neither contributed, nor did they participate in the celebrations on that day.

Before Easter itself, on Good Friday, there was a service throughout the day. When I was attending primary school, and then the convent school in our village, it was obligatory to attend the Good Friday service. One of the teachers would say the prayers out of a book, dragging it out into a chant. Sometimes it turned into a monotonous tune. Really it used to send us all off to sleep. But as usual, one could not drop off to sleep quietly, because of the Sisters' vigilance. Sometimes the Sisters themselves would nod off. But could we go and hit them? Or pinch them?

We'd wear good clothes and put flowers in our hair to go to the Easter midnight service. On that occasion, the Pusai was held in front of the church, outdoors. Everyone would lie down and fall asleep there. The breeze blew through the neem trees and felt fresh and cool. At midnight, when Jesus rose from the dead, the Sisters would wake everyone up, beating them with the mats they sat on. All the bells would ring out then, the big bell in the church tower as well as the small bells used during Pusai. One of the teachers would run up and remove the white cloth which covered the icon of the Risen Christ all this time, and Jesus would stand in front of us, risen from the dead. We would all prostrate ourselves and worship him. As all the bells sounded and the Risen Christ was revealed, I always felt a thrill running through me. It would seem to me that God had truly appeared to us from heaven.

During Pusai they would tell us to light our candles or to put them out at various times. I wanted only to keep mine alight. But the Sisters would not allow it. We had to blow them out. It was fun to make a small heap of earth, plant the candle in it, and play with the flame. The Pusai would proceed on its own course. The priest carried his own big Easter candle. No sooner was the Pusai over than everyone rushed forward carrying spoons and vessels. It most certainly would come to a fight at some point. We'd scoop up some of the new fire and the holy water as best as we could, and then go home.

When we reached home, we had to drink some of the holy water with great devotion, and sprinkle the rest in different places throughout our house. We would place the new fire in the hearth. When we woke up in the morning and made the breakfast idlis, it was that fire that was used to light the cooking stove. Throughout that day we'd cook and eat good meals.

That evening we'd set off from our streets, clapping our hands and beating drums, all the way to the church. There would be a Benediction there. As soon as that was over, the older women would gather in a circle and dance a kummi, singing a hymn which began, *He is coming through our street, Yesu is coming in his chariot.* We'd all gather round to watch the fun. The men would play chadu-gudu. Later, at sunset time, the icon of the risen Lord would be placed in the carrying chariot, decorated, blessed by the priest, and taken in procession through the village.

For some reason the Nadar community would never join in any of this. They never made any contribution towards the festival. They never came forward to decorate the chariot, nor did they offer to carry it. When the procession went along their street, they only peeped at it as the Hindus did, and stayed inside their houses. They never joined in the Dalit celebrations. The procession went along the streets of different communities and castes. All along the way we'd follow singing Christian hymns and saying prayers. We'd go all the way, as far as the bazaar, and go home only after that, to sleep. Only then was Easter over. But I understood what an important event Easter is for us, only after I had left home and gone to study elsewhere. It was only then that I became fully aware of its significance.

Christmas was over for us with the end of the midnight Pusai. It used to be very hard for me to wake up and go to the midnight service at Christmas and Easter. Sometimes, at the very thought of rousing myself from sleep, I would complain, why did this Jesus choose to be born and to rise from the dead at the midnight hour? As a child I preferred Christmas to Easter. Because we were given new clothes at Christmas. But not at Easter. Christmas ended with a customary festive meal of beef.

New Year's Day too was like that. Nowadays, though, the celebration of these festival days is gradually changing. Of course, the change is in keeping with our changing times. But nobody seems to reflect any more on why we celebrate these things. The Sisters and the priests too don't say what needs to be said, but only speak words which are irrelevant, meaningless mumbo-jumbo. Because of all this, these celebrations no longer have any significance for me. What passes for devotion nowadays is merely a matter of doing things out of a sense of duty.

* * * *

When I finished schooling in my village and joined the convent boarding school to study in the ninth class, the fear—bhayam, that I felt towards God gradually left me, and love—paasam, grew. I tried to the best of my ability to pray at all times; to go to Jesus, look at him, and talk to him frequently; not to behave in a way that would cause him pain; not to commit sinful deeds; to be good. There used to be a three-day Retreat every year. I loved it. It was at that time that I began to do such things as going to Pusai every day, receiving Communion, and making a weekly confession with a loving and accepting mind. I really liked the Sisters there. I had a deeply held wish in my heart to become a nun like them and give myself to God. When I finished my exams after the tenth class, I told one of the Sisters about my wish. But she told me that I should only consider it after I had finished my college education.

With difficulty I admitted myself into college. But it was during the time I was studying there that the love and devotion that I felt towards God gradually diminished. Of course, in times of trouble, I thought to myself, God help me, but that was all. Everything became a matter of routine drudgery. All sorts of questions beset my mind, such as, 'Why should I go to Pusai every day? Why should I take Communion?' I began to think that the priests and nuns had deceived me hugely. Up to that time I had thought that God came to me through these people; but this belief changed to the extent that I now began to feel strongly that God was not with them. And so, I began to dislike everything they did. I began to question them. I argued and fought. I thought to myself with some disgust, Chi, they are all hypocrites and frauds.

I felt in my heart that I could go and speak directly to God without their intervention. I could no longer believe that God could only be reached, as they had taught us, through prayer learned by rote, through pious practices, through the novena and the rosary. I came to realize that you could see God through the mind's eye, in nature, and in the ordinary events of every day. So all the rituals that I had followed and believed in so far suddenly began to seem meaningless and just a sham. The desire to become a nun fell away from me entirely at this time.

I finished my education and started to work. By chance I took up a post at a school run by nuns. At the start, when I met them, I thought they would be different in their ways. But as time went on, I realized they were truly like whited sepulchres, as Jesus said. Until I quite realized this, I was even tempted to enter their order and to become one of them. Fortunately I didn't do so.

I worked there for five years. All the children who attended that school were from poor families. About three-fourths of them were from Dalit families. I liked teaching them. I was happy in my fashion. But when I observed some of the atrocities that were going on, I would be ablaze with fury. They could have done so much for those poor children. Instead they ate and lived in comfort and argued amongst themselves.

They ran a boarding school which was nominally for the sake of destitute children, but in fact they made those children do every menial task that was needed. They behaved as if they were the queens there, and everybody else was there only to run errands for them. The few nuns who were even slightly humane had a difficult time. And even amongst themselves there were caste divisions, divisions between the rich and the poor, and even divisions over the languages that they spoke.

Besides the usual lessons, they could have educated the Dalit children in many matters, and made them aware of their situation in the world about them. But instead, everything they said to the children, everything in the manner in which they directed them, suggested that this was the way it was meant to be for Dalits; that there was no possibility of change. And mainly because of this, those children seemed to accept everything as their fate. From dawn to dusk they toiled away in the convent. As I saw all this, I became very troubled at heart. I was angry; I thought to myself, what sort of nuns are these, they claim that they are helping the poor and the needy, yet this is how they are. At times I confronted them and argued with them.

Yet, even though I observed these nuns and their way of life, from time to time I was still seized with a wish to enter an order. I wanted to become a nun, but to be different; I felt a yearning to treat these children as all children ought to be treated, to look after them rather than torment and exploit them. At the same time, I kept on telling myself obstinately that I ought not ever to enter a convent. I continued to cherish in my heart a certain love and devotion towards Jesus and Our Lady. But I found what the nuns and priest said distasteful. Occasionally, when a priest from other parts came and addressed us about our society and about the needs of our people, I would feel an eagerness within me. And it was during those days that I was suddenly seized by a desire to read the Bible through, at least once. So morning and evening, I read my way through the Old Testament and the New Testament.

I learnt that God has always shown the greatest compassion for the oppressed. And Jesus too, associated himself mainly with the poor. Yet nobody had stressed this nor pointed it out. All those people who had taught us, had taught us only that God is loving, kind, gentle, one who forgives sinners, patient, tender, humble, obedient. Nobody had ever insisted that God is just, righteous, is angered by injustices, opposes falsehood, never countenances inequality. There is a great deal of difference between this Jesus and the Jesus who is made known through daily pieties. The oppressed are not taught about him, but rather, are taught in an empty and meaningless way about humility, obedience, patience, gentleness.

I truly don't know what happened to me, in spite of all my criticism of the nuns. More and more the thought grew in my mind that I should become a nun, and teach those who suffer that there is a Jesus who cares, to put heart into them and to urge them onwards. At the same time, I was also aware that even if I became a nun, I might never be allowed to act in this way. All the same, however hard I pushed it away, the idea grew stronger. Sometimes I was even embarrassed that I should harbour such a notion after all these years of criticizing and reproaching the nuns.

When I discussed my plan at home and with my close friends, not one of them supported me. Everyone thought I was joking, I wasn't being serious. I myself wished I could be free of the notion. But the more I hoped to be free of it, the greater grew the urge to enter an order. So, in spite of all the people who advised me against it, in spite of some of them downright forbidding me to do it, I resigned from my job and prepared to enter a religious order. Today I realize what an extremely foolish thing I did. But at that time I didn't understand in the least what I was doing. I was like one who was falling into a well, blindfolded.

In the end I was disappointed by the order that I entered. But to begin with, the first three years were not quite like that. To some extent at least we read and studied about people's hardships and suffering, and about the human attributes of Jesus. We discussed these things. We thought with some urgency about what we ought to do and how we should do it. Time passed, full of the bright imagined hope of what we might achieve after we became nuns. We read about the woman who founded our order. It was good to learn of her love and concern for the poor, and of how she lived and died for their sake. I felt an unshakeable desire to be like her, to suffer for the sake of the poor then and in the future.

At that time, all my prayers, my meditation, and my thoughts were directed towards oppressed and exploited people, and towards the Jesus who fought for justice and fairness. It seemed to me it was meaningless to repeat prayers in beautiful and decorative language, and to live without that correspondence and connection between prayer, worship, and life. I talked to others about my convictions. When there did not seem to be this connection, I asked why it wasn't there. We should never believe one thing and do another. We should speak up about what we believe, and act according to that. That is being true to oneself. Everything else is play-acting. I never cared to survive by acting out a role.

I made my first vows with many hopes and thoughts in my heart. I dreamt that I would share my life with the poor and the suffering, live and die for them. Instead, I was sent to a prestigious school, and asked to teach there. It was only after I arrived there that it all became clear to me. All the children there came from wealthy families. The convent too was a well-endowed one. And the Jesus they worshipped there was a wealthy Jesus. There seemed to be no connection between God and the suffering poor. Neither the prayers that were said morning and night, nor the daily Pusai, showed any evidence of that connection. I couldn't make it out at all. I found I had to search hard to find God.

There was no love to be found in that convent, among these people who declared all the time that God is loving. There was no love for the poor and the humble. They claimed that God's love is limitless, subject to no conditions. Yet inside the convent there were innumerable conditions about how you should be and who you were in order to deserve their love. When outsiders arrived, flaunting their wealth and education, they were treated with one sort of love; if they did not have these things, they were treated in quite a different way, and I am not sure there was any love at all in this case. They shout themselves hoarse that God is just, they sing to this effect in their hymns. But it is injustice that dances like a demon in the convents, and within all the institutions that are run by these people. They say with melting hearts, Our God is a forgiving God. But if you look within, they seem to go about always saying, Who is it, When and what is it, Hit him, Punish him. Their very words are barbed, like arrows. Nobody who gets in the way of their own convenience is let off easily.

With such an ecstasy of devotion they claim in church that God was born into a poor family, lived among the poor, and died poor. But if by accident a poor and lowly person appears within the precincts of the convent or the school, they'll fall upon that person like rabid dogs. On such occasions, I would remember the line, 'It is a sin to treat someone according to their outward appearance.' But then, they have used this very line often enough for their hour-long and special meditations.

In the same way, they hold wonderful expositions on the words of Jesus, that we should take no thought of what we eat or drink. But this is all inside the church and at church meetings. Elsewhere they will discuss for hours about what we should eat today and what we should eat tomorrow, what we should wear. I became completely confused in my head about the place of belief and devotion in all this. There seemed to be one God within the church and another outside. I was extremely bewildered by all these different versions of God. But they seemed to have no problem either with creating these different versions or with juggling smartly between all of them. You have to admit, it takes a kind of skill.

Either they should come out with it and say, yes ours is a God who serves the rich, we follow him and worship him alone, and live openly like that. Otherwise they must say ours is a God of the poor, who chose to be born in a cattle-shed, we too are like him, and then try to live in that way. But there is something ugly in saying one thing and doing another. How long can one play-act in this way? Anyway it wasn't possible for me. I could only leave the order and return into the world. And I don't know if they have become so habituated to their play-acting that they can no longer distinguish between the role and the reality.

Nowadays, now that I have left the order, I am angry when I see priests and nuns. Until I actually entered the convent, I truly did not understand their approach, nor any of their procedures. It was only after my sojourn with them that I understood the lack of humanity in their piety. They speak in an empty way of devotion, renunciation, the Holy Spirit, God's vocation, poverty, chastity, and obedience; they lead lives which remind me only of the Pharisees, Saducees, and High Priests who appear in the Bible. If Jesus were to appear today he would question them much more sharply and severely than he did before. And even if he were to do so, I am not sure whether they will understand.

When I look at the Church today, it seems to be a Church made up of the priests and nuns and their kith and kin. And when you consider who they are, it is clear that they are all from upper castes. They are the ones who are in the positions of power. Yet when you consider the Christian people as a whole, most of them are lowly people and Dalits. These few assume power, control the dispossessed and the poor by thrusting a blind belief and devotion upon them, and by turning them into slaves in the name of God, while they themselves live in comfort.

In the name of God they actually rob from the poor who struggle for their very livelihood. They teach them to shut their eyes when they pray, with the deliberate intention that they should not open their eyes and see. They teach them to shackle their arms together and to prostrate themselves in prayer at full length on the ground so that they should never stand tall. What kind of piety can this be? They make themselves into gods so that they can exploit others. So where has God gone, I wonder? The so-called gods walking about here are the priests and nuns and their relations, no other.

How long will they deceive us, as if we are innocent children, with their Pusai and their Holy Communion, their rosary and their novena? Children, growing up, will no longer listen to everything they are told, open-mouthed, nodding their heads. Dalits have begun to realize the truth. They have realized that they have been maintained as the stone steps that others have trodden on as they raised themselves up. They have become aware that they have been made slaves in the name of God, the Pusai, and the Church. They have experienced a state of affairs where, in the name of serving the poor, these others have risen in power while actually treading on the poor. Dalits have learnt that these others have never respected them as human beings, but bent the religion to their benefit, to maintain their own falsehoods.

But Dalits have also understood that God is not like this, has not spoken like this. They have become aware that they too were created in the likeness of God. There is a new strength within them, urging them to reclaim that likeness which has been so far repressed, ruined, obliterated; and to begin to live again with honour, self-respect, and with a love towards all humankind. To my mind, this alone is true devotion.

Eight

I was born in a small village as a Dalit girl, I grew up, I studied, I worked for five years, and then, as I have said before, I entered a convent. Before I entered it, though, I read about the woman who founded that order. When I learnt how this woman had loved the poor and the lowly, with what steadfastness she had educated the children of the poor and helped them to go forward, I was greatly drawn towards her. I entered the convent with a deeply felt desire that I too should do my utmost to live my life usefully and meaningfully.

It was only after I had joined that I became aware of the true state of affairs there, very gradually, and little by little. Both family members and others whom I knew outside my home had done their best to dissuade me. They had warned me that once inside, I would find that everything was different from the claims that were made. It was I who went in, dreaming that I was about to achieve something tremendous. It was only after I had entered the convent that I came to realize that what they had warned me about was entirely true. But I stayed, thinking to myself, well let me try and deal with this as best as I can.

The convent was a world in itself. We talked a great deal. We spoke about Lord Jesus, Our Lady, the disciplines of the order. At due times we ate good meals. We muttered our prayers according to our discipline. We celebrated this holy day and that; we feasted throughout the day on such occasions. There was such a variety of good things then that one could not make up one's mind what to eat and what to forego. Often, I didn't even know the names of these good things. And if I did, I couldn't even pronounce those names. The comforts and conveniences were such.

If the food was like this, the buildings were even better. All the people of my community from my village could have lived there. It was such a huge convent building, such a big school. I felt very strange about it. I felt a kind of shame. At the same time I felt as if I had gone into a Naicker house. I couldn't act or speak, or even eat independently. That was my feeling.

Then, was there the chance that you could just eat and sleep and go about your own business? Not a bit of it. There were such arguments and dissensions going on within. There were such jealousies, such competition, such arrogance that one could only survive by one's own strategies, guile, and cunning. People accused you of thinking thoughts that you had not thought, of speaking words that you had not spoken. Until you made your final vows you had to run about like a young child, dance to everyone's tune, take upon your own head every menial task which they pushed at you with their feet. I became fed up with it. I asked myself, was this why I chose to come here? I too have my own goal, I thought, I came here for the sake of my people; let these others go their own way.

In time I realized there was no real possibility of this. Always the discussion was at the level of what to prepare, what to eat, what to celebrate and how to enjoy, what to build and what to break, what to buy where and how to sell it. That was all. They never asked, why do people suffer, what is the state of this country, what did Lord

Jesus actually do for people, why did we become nuns, how can we undo these injustices. Such questions never came out of their mouths.

Although the convent was so well-endowed, every time we went home on leave, we were expected to bring back some kind of gift. Was it possible for me to bring anything that would be appropriate to their status and position? Did we have such wealth or property? If someone brought them fancy gifts, whatever seemed appropriate to the convent's style of life, they made much of that person. If not, nobody took the slightest notice of who and what you were. There was definitely a special value attached to someone from a wealthy family, with influence among the upper castes. Otherwise, nobody bothered to come near you.

If you are inclined to think, well all right, the convent was like this, but at least the school would have been good, I have to say, no, actually it was worse. Each class was full of children from wealthy families. They sat in rows, sleek and well-fed. All they had to do was to be light-skinned and to arrive in cars. Even the smallest children would eat meals that were brought to them by servant boys and girls, and whom they grandly ordered around.

As a token gesture they took four or five poor children into the school. These wretches usually shunned the rich ones and lurked in corners, trembling. Every now and then there would be complaints about them. The rich children would say, We don't want to sit next to these ones, they are dark-skinned, they are poor, they are ugly, they don't wear nice clothes. Even in a play or a dance performance the rich children didn't want to put on the costume of the poor. It seemed to me that it was a waste of my time to teach such children. I couldn't speak of this to the others in the convent. Had I spoken about it, they wouldn't, in any case, have listened to me.

As soon as we woke up in the morning there were prayers and Pusai; there were prayers at midday, and in the evening and at night; prayers throughout the day. But there was no connection between these prayers, the life we led, and the work we did. On the one hand, all these prayers were said only as a duty. On the other, such power and status that can't ever be described as truly Christian.

The nuns are required to make three vows, of poverty, chastity, and obedience. They teach that these vows liberate them and enable them to lead lives that are centred around ordinary people. But in truth, the vows become a means of control and enslavement.

When I was outside, I had experienced poverty, and had lived among those who suffered from poverty. But inside the convent I could not see even the traces and tracks of poverty. We could only go round and round, always within our luxurious cages, trapped in comfort.

They spoke so eloquently that we should love everyone, for we are all God's children. Yet the people they chose to talk to, those whom they admitted into their schools, those with whom they claimed relationships were all rich. If we should challenge them about this, they say in explanation that God's calling is not just for the poor; the wealthy too are God's children. They explain that God had said, 'The poor are with you always.' You have to wonder whether you should laugh or cry.

They go on and on about the vow of 'obedience' and force us into submission so that we can scarcely lift up our heads. We are not even allowed to think for ourselves in a way that befits our years. They want to think for us, and instead of us. We are not allowed the independence and rights that even small children are entitled to. When I thought to myself, towards the end of my time with them, never mind, let it all go, and asked only to be sent to a village or anywhere to a school with ordinary and poor children, they intimidated me by talking of 'obedience' and 'faith'. They insisted I could go only where I was sent, I must only do as I was told. They exhorted me to see with the eyes of faith. All I could see was their authority flying high like a flag. People like me were to be sacrificed in order to maintain it. I simply could not understand how I could see all this with the eyes of faith.

In fact all three vows of theirs serve only to separate them from ordinary people, and the reality of ordinary lives, to put them at a great remove, as if they belonged to a different world.

There is a lengthy training and preparation before one becomes a nun and decides to stay in the convent. What they taught us at that time was truly admirable. They told us each one of us is different, each is unique, there is no one else at all like us in the whole world. It was good to hear that God created each one of us in a very special way.

But when it came to actual practice, it was not like that at all. They expected us to behave as if we had all been made from the very same mould. Nobody was allowed to think differently or speak differently. We had to accept only what our Superior told us, as if it were God-given Scripture. If you didn't accept it, or spoke differently, then that was the end of you. They said there was something wrong about your childhood, some gross mistake in your upbringing. They said there was some fatal flaw in your family, as if they were looking at your horoscope.

And what is more, in the end they discovered that 'obedience' and 'humility' did not apply to you because God had not called you after all. In all, it seems as if they wanted to change us to fit various ideas into which they had been indoctrinated during their studies in Europe and in America. If we could not fit within the framework that they had devised, then they concluded that it was doubtful whether we truly had a vocation. We had to change. In the final analysis, we could not be ourselves. They wanted you to be destroyed utterly and remade in a new form. Where else can you find such madness?

Many people in the convent did not even know what was meant by Dalit. And those few who knew had an extremely poor opinion about Dalits; they spoke ill of us. When they spoke about Dalits in such terms, I would often shrink into myself. They did not know then that I myself was a Dalit, and in those early days, I did not have the courage to tell them. I was afraid of how they might talk to me or behave towards me if I told them. When I heard them speak in such a way about the oppressed Dalit people, I used to wonder how these people could bring into being God's kingdom where there are neither the high nor the low.

Some of the things they said about Dalits:

'How can we allow these people to come into our houses? In any case, even if we were to allow them, they would not enter our homes. They themselves know their place.'

'There is nothing we can do for these creatures. And we shouldn't do anything for them. Because to do so would be like helping cobras.'

'Even if we were to do something for them, they will never make progress. Their natures are like that.'

'These days these people go about reasonably dressed. So you can't even make out who they are, sometimes.'

'The government goes and gives these people all sorts of privileges. Why do illiterate people need all these things?'

If ever they had to speak about something unpleasant or ugly, they tended to categorize it as Harijan. What service can people with such tainted minds render? And all the time, my conscience kept hurting me that although I heard, observed, and experienced all this, I too lived a privileged life like an upper-caste person.

After three years, I was transferred to a different place. Then, within a month I was asked to move five times. They assured me that all this was done because they were guided by the Spiritus Sanctus. Only I couldn't understand why, in that case, the Spiritus Sanctus was so indecisive.

Well, I hoped that after all the moves and uncertainty, there would be a firm decision at last to place me in a small school or village. But instead, in the end, they sent me to teach in yet another big school for wealthy children. I was shattered. Was God's calling necessary, I wondered, to take up this meaningless task of being a teacher to rich children, to help them get ahead? It struck me more and more that I might as well be a teacher in the outside world in that case. In that school I would have to act according to the rich children's demands. In fact the entire school was ruled by their demands. When you questioned this, you found out that the convent's income came largely from this source. So it seems one just had to close one's eyes and allow oneself to be dragged along.

I thought to myself, how can you run a school just for profit? Their justification was that from the income they made out of this school, they could do real service elsewhere. When I said, Well, you get on with making your profit, only send me elsewhere and amongst real people, once again I was intimidated with talk of 'obedience' and 'faith'.

For some five months at this school, I gritted my teeth and gave it a try. I couldn't brave it out after that. For how long can you live in disguise? For how many days can oil and water stay mixed together? In the sixth month I decided I couldn't stand the torture any more, packed my box and walked out of the convent. The Lord only knows what I went through before I managed to do that. Nor would they let me go that easily. Somehow I struggled through it all and came home at last. And my difficulties since my return have not been trifling ones either.

Nine

After I dared at last to leave the convent, it was as if I had arrived at a place where I had no connections. Having sheltered within the safety of the convent, eating at regular meal times and living a life with every comfort, I am now in the position of having to endure the hardships of being alone in the outside world, and of having to seek work, and even food and drink for myself.

I feel afraid of everyone and of everything. I feel awkward and strange about going anywhere. The task of finding a job seems monstrously difficult. I can only attempt to do that by looking through the papers and answering job advertisements. Have I the means to bribe my way into a job? Nor do I have anyone who can use their influence on my behalf.

I got an interview at one place, after I answered an advertisement in a newspaper. I went. After I had answered a thousand and one questions, and even written an exam, I was told that the job would fetch me a salary of four hundred rupees a month. At today's prices, in which corner of the world can you survive on four hundred rupees? In any case, I didn't get that job. Why? Because I am a Dalit. It was a school that is governed and run by the Nadar. It seems they only appoint Nadar women. I don't know why, in that case, they make such a fuss about the interview, and invite us all to apply. If they had made it plain in the paper that the job was available only to Nadars, why would I have gone for it?

So it seems that Nadar schools only admit Nadars, and Naicker schools only admit Naickers. And then, Aiyar schools will only teach Aiyar children. If it is all like this, then heaven knows where all the Dalit children can go and break their heads. I don't know if there is such a thing as a Dalit school.

Then, if Dalits accept that nobody else will take any notice of them, and ask for admission in the schools run by Catholic nuns and priests, they are told that if they take Dalit children, their standards will fall. They marginalize all of us Dalits as being of poor quality. Amongst all this, it is a real dilemma where and how I can find a job and survive.

I grow older all the time. Can one sit at home, unemployed, uselessly eating one's meals? Perhaps it might just be possible, so long as one's parents are alive. After their time, what is there of one's own? Who? My siblings have their own lives to lead. And for how long can even close friends help out?

If it is so difficult even to find a means of living, there is also another great difficulty, the difficulty I find in moving about in the outside world, alone. If a woman so much as stands alone and by herself somewhere, all sorts of men gather around her showing their teeth. However angry you get, however repelled by their expressions and their grimaces, even to the point of retching, what can you do on your own? We think so many thoughts. We hope so much. We study so many things. But in real life everything turns out differently. We are compelled to wander about, stricken and unprotected.

It is really very hard to return to a life in this world after seven or eight years of hiding away from reality. You can sit on your chair inside a convent, and say whatever you like about the struggling masses, about justice and the law. You can pray for the good of this group or that, while continuing to live in comfort. But in that place you can never experience other people's pain.

But now, here, I do experience it. Today I do know what it is to be hungry, to suffer illness in solitude, to stand and stare without a paisa in one's hand, to walk along the street without protection, to be embarrassed by a lack of appropriate clothes, to be orphaned and entirely alone, to swim against the tide in this life without position or status or money or authority. But I have never once regretted that I left the convent with all its comforts and conveniences. In any case, that was for me a counterfeit existence. Always, all the time, I had to assume a false position in front of others. And how is it possible to wear a disguise all twenty-four hours?

When I was in the convent, it always seemed to me that we were alienated from ordinary people and that ordinary people had become foreigners to us. And this was because we had a number of elitist attributes such as status, money, and a comfortable life, and so they never could be close to us. But now that I have nothing of my own, and because I am exactly like them, they are able to talk to me in a much more familiar way. And I can behave towards them in a perfectly normal manner.

I don't know what kind of magic it is that they work upon us in the convent, but during these seven or eight years, my brain has become confused and dulled. In some ways, they actually change you into a different person. It was this change that seemed to hinder me from being able to live again. By being told all the time to repress this and renounce that thought, to act like this, to be like this, eventually we become strangers even to ourselves. Because I had been caged within that special world, it was difficult, when I came outside to find a way of dealing with the energy of the real world. The strategy of the convent had been to transform my identity completely.

At the time that I entered the convent, I was like the strong core of a teak tree. Both in mind and in body, I was as firm and steadfast as that. But when I came out, I had lost all my strength, and was as feeble as a murunga tree that blows over in the wind. It was only after I entered the convent that I fell prey to every illness and disease. My mind too had been buffeted and knocked about, so that I was only living a half-life or a quarter-life. In such a diminished state, how could I be of service?

I don't know by whose grace or blessing it was, but I did come to my senses; I came out into the world. And although it is so hard to make a living, yet I am truly happy to live with a whole and honest mind. I feel a certain contentment in leading an ordinary life among ordinary people. I can breathe once again, independently and at ease, like a fish that has at last returned to the water, after having been flung outside and suffered distress. I have entirely lost faith in all that talk of service to the poor from within the convent. It is possible to live in elitist style with money, education, authority and power, and to claim that one is serving the poor. But what kind of service is it that is done without humanity?

Now, many thoughts come crowding to me. I am like a bird whose wings were broken. After its wings have been broken, it is protected only if it stays within its cage. But if it comes out, it can only flap its wings uselessly, unable to fly. And that is the state in which I am now.

With all their words and rules in the convent, they cut me down, sculpted me, damaged me. Today I blunder and stumble about in the world outside. Most of all, it hurts me that I should be doing this at my age.

I don't know when my wings will heal and gain enough strength so that I too will be able to fly again. Just as people throw sticks and stones to wound a wingless bird, many people have wounded me with their words and deeds. Yet I know I'm moving forward slowly, step by step.

Those people who stuck with me in my prosperous days have torn themselves away and gone. A few who heard of my present distress have come to me on the pretext of wishing to help and heal, but have merely stirred the wound; they too have left. Yet with all the pain, there still is a certain happiness in the depths of my mind. I have courage, I have a certain pride. I do indeed have a belief that I can live, a desire that I should live.

For the time being, I cannot see my way ahead. Yet I believe it is possible to live a meaningful life, a life that is useful to a few others. I comfort myself with the thought that rather than live with a fraudulent smile, it is better to lead a life weeping real tears.

Postscript

After I became a nun, I worked for three years, as teacher of Mathematics at a school in Madras. At the end of the third year, I heard that I was to be transferred to another convent. It seemed to me that it would be good if they moved me to a convent in a small village, in a rural area. But Sister Lily, who was also at the same convent with me said that they were not likely to send me to a place of my choice, but only where my service was required. I didn't care to continue teaching in the same way as before, but what could I do? Anyway, it seemed to me that it wouldn't be too bad if I were sent to a village. Well, I thought, I would wait and see where they would transfer me.

By the end of April, the exams were over and we were on leave. In the first week of May, the Provincial spoke to me on the telephone and told me that I was selected to become the head teacher at a village school near Madurai. Although I was happy that it was to be a village school, I felt rather strange at the thought of becoming a head teacher. It was quite a big school, many of the teachers would be older than me. I wasn't too happy about becoming their head. They could have recruited me as an ordinary teacher. Why this? I was still only a junior Sister. It astonished me that they had chosen me to be a head teacher.

Had it been a senior Sister who had made her Final Vows already, she might have commanded some respect. I was in a quandary.

While I was in this state of confusion, another telephone call came for me from the Provincial. This time she said that I needn't go to the school she had mentioned originally, but that I should stay in Madras and go to another school as a Maths teacher. I agreed to this as well. But I knew that if it was going to be in Madras, it would be yet another school attended by children from wealthy families. I told one of the other Sisters about this second decision. I said that instead of my staying here, it would have been better if I had been sent to a village school. Hearing this, she told me, 'I heard that that was what they decided at first. But it seems our Councillor Sister Marian argued hotly against sending you there, and got them to change their minds.'

'And why was that?'

'She asked how they could choose a junior Sister as a head teacher, and maintained stubbornly that they should never do that. It seems that so far, in this Order, they have never given such a post to a junior Sister. Anyway, after that, they found out that a Maths post was vacant here, and decided to transfer you to it.'

'But they could have made me an ordinary Maths teacher at the village school, couldn't they?'

'You have nearly ten years' experience, haven't you? That's why they all wanted you to be the head teacher there. But it was this one Sister who didn't want it. Do you know why? She doesn't like Tamizh nuns. If they had chosen someone from her community, she wouldn't have minded. Just look at this, out of your set, they've only chosen Sister Rita to study medicine and become a doctor. That's because, Rita is related to Marian. Although Sister Edna had higher marks than Rita, she wasn't chosen. Edna was really upset and told me about it. What can we do? We have to go where they send us. There's no other way.'

I didn't say anything. My heart was heavy. I had been told that I should be at my new post by the end of May. So I had made everything ready. But then, a third telephone call came from the Provincial. This time she said, 'You don't have to take up the post of Maths teacher at the school in Madras. Go instead to our Teacher Training School. Your service is needed there.'

I didn't know whether to laugh or cry. It irritated me that they were changing their decision like this, every other day. How many times was I to ready myself for a new task? I told myself that hereafter I should have no expectations nor make any forward plans. I didn't want to talk to anyone about any of this. In the midst of all this the Principal of the school in which I had been working summoned me and said, 'Why couldn't they have left you here instead of transferring you to another school in Madras as a Maths teacher? Why such a needless transfer? I am not going to let you go. You just stay on here. Let them send someone else there.'

'No, Sister. They have changed their decision yet again, and I've been told to go to a Teacher Training School.'

She shouted angrily, 'My God! Why are they tormenting you like this? You tell them you won't go anywhere, you'll just stay on here.'

I didn't say anything. The very next day there was another telephone call from the Provincial. Now she said, 'I have transferred you to Jammu, in the state of Jammu and Kashmir. I have informed your Superior already. Be ready to leave by the first week of June.'

After such a distressing time, my mind was tossing as if it were in a storm, not knowing whether I should agree to go or not. I wondered if I should just leave everything and go home. At the same time I wondered if I shouldn't just give it a try, and go to Jammu. My journey would take me through Delhi. I made up my mind that I would see the Provincial in person when I was there, and tell her plainly how I felt. So I left. But once I reached Jammu, it was clear to me that I absolutely could not stay on. Each day I spent there was as if I was standing in the midst of a fire. The Sisters there wouldn't even talk to me. They would only talk amongst themselves. They took no notice of me, whatever. The Mother Superior there would only tell me what my tasks were, nothing else. I didn't want to waste my life any longer. I began to feel that I should leave the place, come what may. It seemed to me that I could only be at peace outside the convent. So, after many days of hesitation and lack of clarity, I came to the decision, finally, that I must definitely leave the convent and go out into the world.

Once I had made up my mind to leave the convent, I told the Mother Superior there. She said to me I couldn't just leave the convent according to my whim, that there were certain procedures that had to be followed, that I would have to inform the head of our Order in India first of all, and that she would start the appropriate proceedings. I replied that in that case, could she please inform the Provincial. She said that the Provincial was not in India just then, she was attending a meeting elsewhere, she would be back in a week. She would be informed of all this upon her return.

But another Sister there told me, 'They won't let you go as easily as you imagine. You will only manage to go by your own effort. Don't think they will send you away willingly. That's not going to happen.'

'I don't like it here, I want to go. How can they prevent me?'

'You are simply not aware of all the details. They will take into consideration that you are a teacher with a lot of experience, and that you will be useful to them in running their schools really well; so they won't let you go easily. Besides, you finished all your studies on your own, and were already an experienced teacher before you joined the order; that was very convenient as far as they were concerned. I'm just telling you.'

It seemed to me that what she said was fair enough. So I wrote to a friend and asked him to send me five hundred rupees immediately. The money arrived within a week. It was quite a problem for me to collect it from the postman. I had to inform him without letting anyone else know, calculate the time of his arrival, run into the garden, take it from him, and hide it away. I was quite exhausted by the end of it all. I asked the Sister who put the idea into my head in the first place, to accompany me, and went to the railway station, giving the excuse that we were just going to the shops. There I made enquiries, and bought a ticket which would take me directly to Tiruchi. That train, I found, only left once a week. If it left Jammu on a Friday night, it would arrive at Tiruchi only on Monday night. Because of the heavy demand, it was difficult to get a ticket on it. Even though I wanted to leave as soon as possible, it was difficult to get a ticket immediately. I enquired in early October, but could only get a ticket for 8 November. After I had come away with the ticket, I waited and waited, desperate for the date to come round.

Meanwhile, I heard that the Provincial had returned to India, and went again to our Mother Superior with my request. She replied, handing me ten or twelve cassettes, 'I have talked to her about your problem. She advises you to think very carefully before you come to a decision. Here, take these cassettes, listen to them, reflect and meditate, and then decide.'

'I have reflected well before coming to my decision. I have even bought my ticket, now. I shall leave on 8 November. That's all. There's nothing more for me to consider,' I said, and came away.

The next day Mother Superior summoned me, and spoke quietly and lovingly. 'After speaking to you the other day, I telephoned the

Provincial that very evening. She said she wants to speak to you directly, before you leave the convent. So please hand me your ticket home, and take the train to Delhi this very night. If, after you have spoken to her, you still want to leave, you may certainly do so.'

I reported all this, word for word, to the Sister who had accompanied me to the station. What she said in reply really frightened me. 'Sister, please do not ever hand your ticket to her, for any reason whatsoever. If you do, you are done for. You'll never be able to go home. They'll pluck the ticket from you hands and never give it back. And another thing: please don't go and see the Provincial. If you go there, you will never come back again.'

'Why? What can they do to me? What is this, Sister, you are frightening me!'

'I don't want to scare you; I'm only telling you the truth. Do you happen to know Sister Sangeetha? She was summoned just like this, and then was kept under what amounted to house arrest. They made sure she could not contact anyone outside. She at least was a bold type of person. If people like you get caught, you'll just have to stay there. That's why I'm telling you. Keep your ticket with you at all times. They will do their best to grab it from you. Be quite watchful until you leave.'

After this, I went about everywhere with the ticket safely in my possession. When I told the Mother Superior that I would not go to Delhi to see the Provincial, she reacted angrily at first, but controlled herself, and asked patiently, 'Why are you refusing to go? Are you scared of going by yourself? Very well then, come, we'll both go. We'll go today to see her, and will return by tomorrow night's train. Do you agree?'

I shook my head, meaning No. Her anger mounted. She shouted, 'Why won't you come with me? If a Superior summons you, a junior has to obey. Besides, when the Mother Superior summons you, how dare you shake your head? You will certainly come with me. We *have* to go.'

I didn't go, however much she shouted. Two days later she sent for me, and asked me to write a letter to Mother General. I had no idea what I should write. But an elderly Sister who had joined us from another convent advised me on what I should say. She told me to ask that I be released from the three vows of poverty, chastity, and obedience, which I had undertaken when I became a nun, and sent home from the convent. I wrote the letter according to her instructions, and handed it in. Mother General was away in some foreign country at the time. They kept telling me that I could not leave until I had received her letter of release. But inwardly, I was counting the days. I was determined to flee from that place, whether the letter arrived in time or not.

I informed the friend who had sent me the money that I would arrive in Tiruchi on the night of 11 November. I asked him to please find me a teaching post in any school. He replied that he had spoken to a nun, and was arranging some employment for me. I felt that first of all, and by every means, I should look for work. Once I was employed, I need not depend on anyone for anything.

As the days passed by, I was scared, too. I didn't know where I should go or what I should do, once I left the convent. I really wanted to leave. But I wasn't in a fit state of mind to consider what my life was going to be, thereafter. Just as strongly as I felt when I first wanted to join a convent and become a nun, I now struggled with an insistent sense that I must leave. Each day I was there felt as if I was sitting on thorns. The same mind that stubbornly held out against all the advice from my family that I should not become a nun, now told me just as stubbornly, that I must leave. I couldn't understand anything. On the one hand I felt that if I got away from there, that would be enough. At the same time I wondered whether everyone would hold me in contempt if I went home now.

'Well, let them,' I thought. 'I mustn't go home directly. I should go there only after I have found some sort of job in Madurai. If I go there empty-handed, having thrown away the work I had, everyone will point their fingers at me and talk about me maliciously. And not just me, they will speak about my parents too, in a humiliating and shameful way. Anyway, I shouldn't appear to be totally downhearted and anxiety-ridden, either. Somehow or the other, I should return to the old life that I left off; but I must show that I am able to live even better than before. Most importantly, I must let my mother see that I am happy. Otherwise she will worry excessively. As it is, she is in poor health. She mustn't be made unhappy by the sight of me. In that home she is the one soul who loves me truly.' At the very thought of her, the tears flooded down my cheeks. I wiped them away, and continued with my thoughts for a long time.

'What will I do, if I don't get a job? No, but I must find something, anything at all, somehow or other. It will be the end of me if I sit at home doing nothing. I should not go and be a burden to them in their old age. My father is likely to speak impulsively and hurtfully. He will say that had I listened to him when he wanted to get me married, I wouldn't be in this state now. If I sit at home with nothing to do now, he might even start talking to me once again about getting married. At that time at least, I was brave enough to resist him and oppose the idea. Now I won't be in a position to do that. Now they are sure to treat me like a criminal. It is possible to talk to Amma; but Appa will never listen to her. The only solution is to stay away from home. I shouldn't go anywhere near them until I have some kind of employment. At least then I'll have the courage to say that I can live by myself and earn my own livelihood. Yes, but can I really live all alone by my own earnings, for the rest of my life? But I must do so. If I get married just because I am afraid of being alone, I will land myself in far greater trouble. On the other hand, if I do marry, even if it is a difficult life, I'd at least have a companion. Yes, but what kind of company would that be? If I were to marry, I would have to live the rest of my life and even die in the end for the sake of one man. What use would I be then, to society? Wasn't it in the belief that my life should be useful to others, however few, that I joined the convent? In just the same way, even though I leave the convent now and go into the outside world, I want to show that it is possible to live a life that is at least a little useful to society.'

By the beginning of November, I had packed up all my things. It wasn't as if I had a lot of goods I could take away. I was told I must return all the saris I had worn as a nun. If I had kept them, they would have been of no use to me, anyway. The Sister who helped me buy my ticket was the one who looked after all the finances of the convent. She went to the shops and bought four coloured saris for me. I packed only these in my case. It was the same sister who took me to the station at evening time on 8 November. Before I left, I said goodbye to the Mother Superior, and all the nuns in the convent. I felt no emotion at all. My heart was inert, it felt no agitation. And it was very heavy. After I climbed into my compartment I felt somewhat at peace.

Before I left the convent, the Mother Superior had said, gazing out of her window, 'Some Sisters will come to meet you at the Delhi station. I have given them your train details and your coach number.'

Her words fell on my ears, but I didn't ask why, or for what reason they wanted to see me. It didn't even strike me to ask her that. I sat there quietly. The train began to pull out. I turned my head and gazed around me at everyone, just once. I gazed at the other travellers sitting beside me thinking…who are these people…what are their lives like? Almost all of them seemed very lively. From their conversation I understood that they were all working for the army, and were on their way home, on leave. What joy there was in their faces! I too was going home…but what was in my heart?

I felt slightly feverish. My head ached. I couldn't weep. I couldn't speak to the others in a normal fashion. This, in spite of the fact that everyone there was a Tamil speaker. When I heard them speak Tamil, I felt consoled, a little. They asked me about myself. I told them, very briefly. When I didn't know, myself, where I was headed, what could I say to them? I just said, Tiruchi. I was happy that by a stroke of luck, they were all getting off the train before me. I thought to myself how good it would be if I could go on travelling, all by myself, without ever getting off.

They ate their evening meal, and invited me to eat, too. I pleaded a fever, and refused. Each of them had brought a crate of apples. They offered me a couple from their store. I accepted them, afraid that they might feel hurt if I did not. I gave them the sandwiches I had with me. They, in turn, accepted these, and ate them. Their happiness lightened my heart a little. They talked for a long time, late into the night. They played cards. At last they fell sleep. I was the only one there who could not sleep. Once again, I thought of home. I lay there thinking random thoughts.

'I must go straightaway to Madurai, after reaching Tiruchi. I must ask that friend whether he has been able to arrange some sort of job for me. It would be good to find something near Madurai or Tiruchi. I mustn't go near my home for a while. As soon as I've found a job I must go and see my mother. She is the one I long to see. Of course she'd be happy to see me, even were I to go straightaway to her, just as

I am. But she'd be stricken, thinking to herself, what's this … she has thrown away her life, and has nothing now.'

I wanted to shout, 'Amma, I haven't thrown away my life; I have rescued it, just as I was about to throw it away, and brought it home safely. I must live a new life now, Amma. I really must.'

When I thought of my father, I felt a great unease. He was sure to say, 'How many times I told you not to enter the convent. Did you listen? Now you've not only lost a secure job, you've grown older as well. Nowadays it's not that easy to find a job, you know. Now what are you going to do?' I mustn't answer him, I told myself. Amma would speak up for me. 'She's only just arrived. She has an education, hasn't she? She'll find something; she'll survive.' Yes, Amma, I thought, I'll survive … Amma, will I survive? I wept as I asked this. I wanted to sob loudly, but for fear of waking the others, I went on crying soundlessly. My head ached more and more. I felt as if my fever had got worse. Tears streaked down my face and into my ears. I sat up and wiped them away. Everyone in the compartment was sound asleep. I longed to fall asleep like the others. Again I lay down.

My thoughts flew about wildly. It grew fiercely cold. I pulled out a bed sheet from my case and covered myself. I thought a blanket would have been comforting. When I thought of the life of comfort and ease in the convent, a slight smile came to my face. I remembered the nights when I lay in bed snugly, with a couple of blankets on top as well as a hot-water bottle beside me. So many kinds of food, so many different vegetables and fruit! Hereafter, the life of ordinary people would be my life too. That would last; that was the reality.

The train arrived at Delhi station at dawn. I gazed at that bustling station without the least interest. Suddenly, two nuns climbed into my compartment. All the other passengers watched eagerly, wondering what was going on. As for me, I blinked at them in shock, feeling utterly drained of strength in my body and mind. The two newcomers showed me a number of documents and asked me to sign them. I signed mechanically in all the places they pointed to, feeling no emotion whatsoever. I felt like a prisoner who had just escaped from a jail. Once they obtained my signature, they left some of the papers with me, climbed down, and went away.

After they left, at last I looked at the documents I had been given. They said that thereafter I had no further connection or dealings with the Order, that I could not claim any money for the work I had done there, and that I was released by the Mother General from the three vows I had made; the papers had her signature. I had to laugh bitterly. The others there asked me what had happened. I told them something or other, passing it off. They knew that I was evading their questions, yet they didn't persist with their questions any longer, and that was a comfort. I spent most of the rest of the time until we arrived at Tiruchi, lying down on the upper berth. I wanted to get off quickly. At the same time I wanted to stay on the train, travelling on and on forever.

I thought it most probable that this would be the last long train journey I would undertake. After this, when would I go to Delhi? My journey towards that convent in Jammu had been an equally arduous one. The Sisters at Delhi had bought me an unreserved ticket, but had put me into me a reserved compartment. They told me that someone they knew on the train would bring me a reservation slip. Nothing of that sort happened. The ticket inspector examined my ticket and began to shout at me in Hindi. I tried and tried to explain in English. He couldn't understand my English; I couldn't understand his Hindi. He gave my suitcase a violent kick with his boots, pushing it away. It hurtled straight towards the toilets and stopped there. Then he dragged me along there, as well. On top of this, he asked me to pay the excess fare. Someone next to me told me that if I paid the excess, I could stay on, otherwise I would have to get off at the next station and make for the unreserved compartment. It scared me to think how I would get off that compartment in the middle of the night and find my way, carrying my luggage. So I paid up the money he asked for, and stayed there by the toilet, with my case. Even now the tears came into my eyes when I remembered how I arrived at that convent in Jammu, my heart full of sorrow.

On this return journey, I felt numb within. I didn't feel that former agony. Now it was as if I stood in the middle of a forest, directionless, having lost my way. I had got on to the train on Friday night. I never once got off it during the entire journey. My body was totally weary, and longed to get off. But my mind yearned to stay on, never leaving the train until I had reached some unknown, unseen country. I stayed on the train for three whole days, Saturday, Sunday, and Monday, arriving at last in Tiruchi on Monday night.

I was reluctant to get off at Tiruchi station. It was at that instant of arrival, that all my pain struck me suddenly and at once, tormenting me. I got off my compartment in agony, and stood there, my suitcase in my hand. A porter came up and asked me if he should carry it for me. I shook my head in refusal, observed the other passengers, and followed them out of the station. Not just the outside world, but all the rest of my life seemed to loom large in front of me. It was as if I was entering a foreign land where I didn't belong. Just as your eyes dazzle when you see a very bright light, my mind felt faint, shocked and dazzled. It was in such a state of mind that I boarded the bus for Madurai.

I climbed into the bus and bought a ticket, but at first I wasn't happy about going on to Madurai. I was confused about what I would do after I reached there. At the same time, I didn't know where else

I should go, if not there. I wondered whether I had made the right decision in coming here. But my heart assured me it was right; it was just that I didn't have any clarity about how to survive hereafter. I had been courageous enough to come out into the world. Now I must seek out a way of living in the world, I thought. I would manage whatever troubles came my way. Very well, I told myself, let me go on to Madurai and meet this friend. I had told him to arrange for some employment for me; he would surely have done so.

I recalled that Amma would say to me often, he who has planted the tree will also water it. In the same way, the Lord would show me the way. Yes, after I found a job, I would be alone. And yes, that is how it had to be. It is now, for the very first time that I must learn to be truly alone. It may be difficult at first, but in due time I would get used to it. I had learnt to live through so many painful experiences. I would see now … My thoughts ran on, at random. I wasn't even aware when we arrived at Madurai. When I realized that everyone in the bus was getting of it, I too climbed out hastily. It was then past ten o'clock at night. I stood there for a while at the bus stand, completely numb. Then I came to myself, thinking I shouldn't stand there at dead of night, like a crazed woman. I picked up my case, walked along to the place where the town bus was standing, boarded it and travelled towards my friend's place. Once again I felt like travelling in that bus forever, without getting off anywhere. At last, when it was past eleven, I reached my destination.

Because I had forewarned him, my friend was waiting for me. There were a few others there with him. By then, my mind was completely empty.

Author's Afterword to the First Edition

Almost seven years after I wrote *Karukku*, I have read it now, in English translation. The emotions that I had felt during its writing, rose up once again, in a great flood. And I could not help but reflect upon many changes that have taken place since then: the turning points in my life during these past seven years, many startling events, sorrows, achievements; my perspectives about my own life and about society.

In 1995, my beloved younger sister met a violent death. Within the very next year, both my parents died, one after the other. Because I live by myself in this society, without support of my own such as a family, a husband, and children, I have to face many problems. But even though there are a thousand difficulties which beset a Dalit woman living on her own, yet the truth is that in my position as an independent woman, there are many opportunities for me to spend my life usefully, and especially, to work for the liberation of Dalits. This fact is both a consolation and an encouragement to me. It is for this reason that the urge grows greater day by day that I should carry quietly in my heart all the sorrows that followed one upon the other, and to live a life that has meaning and dedication.

Each day brings new wounds, but also new understanding, new lessons that experience teaches, sufficient mental strength to rise up even from the edge of defeat. I have seen the brutal, frenzied, and ugly face of society and been enraged by it. But at the same time, I have danced with joy because of the sweetness and simplicity of a life that is in touch with nature. Even though I have walked hand in hand with anxieties, I have also recognized a strength and zest within myself, flowing like a forest stream, and this has refreshed me. So, there have been many healthy contradictions in my life.

I have met several people who work with zeal for the single objective of Dalit liberation. And it has been a great joy to see Dalits aiming to live with self-respect, proclaiming aloud, *'Dalit endru sollada; talai nimirndu nillada'* ('Say you are a Dalit; lift up your head and stand tall'). To see them joining ranks in order to gain political, economic, and cultural strength. To see a fighting spirit gaining ground among people who have been accustomed, throughout the years, to being beaten down. To see them resisting those who have attacked them in an unjust and inhuman way, for so long. At the same time, I have also been crushed by the growing violence, cruelties, and repressive measures directed towards Dalits in recent times. Beyond all this there stands firm a fierce anger that wants to break down everything that obstructs the creation of an equal and just society, and an unshakeable belief in that goal.

I have met many friends during the course of my life's journey. They have shared my sorrows and helped me in all things. They have inspired me to engage in my work with close attention, with an awareness of my responsibility, and an understanding of the community's needs. They have helped me to identify my own strengths, and made me put them to use. Many Dalit women, for whom toil is their very life-breath, who lead vigorous lives in spite of all their weariness and anxieties, have been a great inspiration as well as a constant help to me. I have been restored by the love, friendship, support, and advice of all these people, and enabled to live with fresh courage and resolution.

My love and thanks go to Mini Krishnan, editor at Macmillan and this series, who was keen to publish *Karukku* in English translation, and who made every effort to bring it about, and to Lakshmi Holmström who has translated *Karukku* into English without once diminishing its pungency.

2000   BAMA

Glossary

chadu-gudu	:	the same team game as kabaddi, where members of a team hold their breath and run over to the opposite side, one by one, to try and capture members of the other team.
daavani	:	half-sari
jalli-kattu	:	a sport in which bulls are baited and chased
kanji	:	thin gruel rice or other grains; sometimes just the starchy water drained from cooked rice.
kolam-flour	:	rice or soapstone powder, used for making kolam designs on the flour
kummi	:	folk dance performed by women and girls, with rhythmic clapping
kuuthu	:	folk theatre based on episodes from the epics and puranas
macchaan	:	literally, brother-in-law; more generally a form of address between friends
Marudai	:	Madurai in uneducated speech

Nadar	:	a caste name; in Bama's village Nadars are toddy-tappers and shopkeepers
Naicker	:	a landowning caste, the dominant caste community in Bama's village
padi	:	a measure; the equivalent of 1.5 kilos
pandal	:	a partially enclosed space, erected outdoors
pannaiyaal	:	labourer
pey	:	a minor evil spirit or ghost
pisaasu	:	minor evil spirit or ghost
pullaanguzhal	:	flute
sabai	:	club or society; in *Karukku,* church groups and societies
sapparam	:	small wooden chariot carried on the shoulders in which the icons are taken out in procession at festival times
silambam	:	a martial art or sport, in which staves are used as in fencing
villuppaattu	:	folk performance in which a story is sung to the accompaniment of several musical instruments, particularly the bow-shaped vil

About the Author and the Translator

BAMA is the most acclaimed Dalit woman writer. A former nun, Bama's traumatic experiences on leaving the Convent were recorded in *Karukku* (1992), a self-narration that focuses on caste not only in the Christian community but also in the seminary. This work, which could not find a publisher twenty years ago, is now a classic in the category of Dalit testimonies and made Bama the first-ever Dalit woman writer in Tamil.

Lakshmi Holmström's English translation of *Karukku* won the Crossword Award in 2001 and established Bama as a distinct voice in Indian Dalit literature. Bama's second and third works, *Sangati* (1994) and *Vanmam* (2002) appeared in English translation through OUP. Her short story collection, *Kisumbukkaran* (1996), was translated into English as *Harum-Scarum Saar* by Ravi Shanker (Women Unlimited 2006). Her first two works *Karukku* and *Sangati* have appeared in German, French, Telugu, and Malayalam translations.

Bama works as a high school teacher of Mathematics in Uthiramerur, a small village in Kancheepuram district. After school hours, she spends most of her time talking to young Dalit women about religion, oppression, and social change. Bama published two collections of short stories *Oru Thathavum Erumayum* and *Kondattam* in 2003 and 2009 respectively and in 2012 her fourth full-length work, *Manushi*, a novel.

LAKSHMI HOLMSTRÖM has translated short stories, novels, and poetry by major contemporary writers in Tamil. She received the Crossword Award in 2001, the Iyal Award from the Tamil Literary Garden in 2008, and shared the Crossword-Hutch Award in 2007. Her most recent translations are *Wild Girls, Wicked Words* (Kalachuvada Publications and Sangam House 2012) and *In a Time of Burning* (Arc Publications 2013).